THE MAKING OF ALEX.

At Gaugamela, Alexander (Colin Farrell) and Ptolemy (Elliot Cowan) shout to the retreating Persian king Darius that they will pursue him to the end.

ROBIN LANE FOX

R&L

OXFORD · LONDON

R&L

OXFORD - LONDON

ISBN 0-9511392-1-5
The author asserts the moral right to be identified as the author of this work.

Robin Lane Fox wishes particularly to thank Moritz Borman, Chairman of Intermedia, and Oliver Stone for their encouragement and help with this book. The many who worked with the 'Alexander' film know the exceptional spirit and commitment which characterized it. Such qualities begin from the top and on behalf of all of them the author would like to pay tribute to the tireless dedication and openmindedness of the Director, Oliver Stone.

Special thanks are also due to Thomas Schühly for the origins of the book, important documentary evidence and wide-ranging discussion. The selection and permission for the pictures were kindly organised, like much else, by Dennis Higgins at Intermedia. Colin Farrell, Jared Leto, Jan Roelfs, Jenny Beavan, Jim Erickson, Dale Dye, Ian Beattie and Rosario Dawson were particularly generous with their memories, as were scores of other participants. Tamsin Cox and Gilly Barnard were the crucial typographic and technological experts throughout. Henry Lane Fox and Anne Kehoe made the production possible.

Photographs © 2004 IMF3
Photographer © Jaap Buitendijk, except for photos on pp. 25, 105 and 145 by John Scheele.

Set in Granjon.
Designed by Gilly Barnard at Snowbooks.com, 239 Old Street, London, EC1V 9EY.
Produced by Maxipos.com, 15a Berghem Mews, 156 Blythe Road, London, W14 0HD.
Printed and bound in the UK.

Opposite page: Director Oliver Stone discusses a direction with Alexander (Colin Farrell) during the filming of the Gaugamela battle.

FOREWORD BY OLIVER STONE

For whatever reason, Alexander of Macedon has eluded dramatization for 2,300 years. Often, I've wondered why. I eagerly lined up for the Richard Burton 1956 film, which I loved, along with other Greek epics of the period, such as "Helen of Troy" and "300 Spartans", probably more for their blend of costume, sensual behavior, and worship of strange gods than their success as dramas. It was because the imaginations of the Greeks struck me as daring, whereas the Romans of the period films seemed militaristic, spartan.

Perhaps then there was some elemental Greek curse on this extraordinary young man, about whom we've heard so much and know so little. He is, without doubt, one of the purest dramatic protagonists and paradoxes of ancient times. And yet, not one Greek or Roman, Elizabethan or Victorian has portrayed his life on a stage. Why not?

The story is beautiful - a heroic young man, a dynamic prince, then a king in his time, who struggled mightily with his two strong parents, succeeded them, and achieved many of his dreams on earth. I would say he was the world's greatest idealist and as a result he took the world's greatest fall. A brilliant military commander who never suffered defeat in battle, he risked his life numerous times, yet remained a visionary of remarkable and generous spirit, who sought to live a life modeled on the great mythological Greek figures of Herakles, Dionysus, Achilles and, to my mind, Prometheus. From these beliefs grew his monumental drive and destiny.

He was clearly a man ahead of his time, or some might say, a new definition of man. His vision of reconciling barbarian and Greek races was too much for many Greeks, and made his last years particularly painful. He lost many friends; there were betrayals; his love life was fascinating, as well as heartbreaking; he could be extraordinarily gentle and extravagantly savage. His failures, in the end, towered over most men's achievements. And when you think about it, he actually outdid Herakles and Achilles in his impact on the world - and accomplished this all in 32 years! He made me believe in heroes. And for this, he must be remembered - as an icon, at the very least, of a young person breaking through the barriers of our personal lives. Nor should we overlook, as both students and participants in history, the eternal sense of possibility in Alexander's idealism. Such men are the great invigorators of history.

As a dramatist, in the end I trust my instinct, and I feel he had all the demon-drives which modern people have, and these too should be presented forthrightly. So, I've told his complex life as a 'parallel' story - wherein the younger Alexander exists side by side with the older Alexander. One of the great ironies of his life is that his later actions become such haunted and tragic repercussions of his earlier ones.

To get inside a man who lived 2,300 years ago and changed the nature of the world, I had no better collaborator than Robin Lane Fox, Ancient Historian at Oxford University, who wrote one of the clearest and least-biased biographies of Alexander in 1973. Among the great contributions of this book is its insistence on rigorously stating the known facts in Alexander's life, and dismissing most of what has become acceptable as history. On the internet and often in magazine essays, I'm still surprised to see that some 50% or more of what is said about him is pure tabloid. Thus the myths grow, apart from the truth and yet with a kernel of some truth to them (i.e. 'well, if he wasn't actually bigger than life on such occasion, he should've been!'). The actual historiography of Alexander, the way his history has been constructed through the centuries, is an equally fascinating parallel to his real life.

As his enthusiasm grew and he increasingly participated in our film, all that Robin Lane Fox asked, in return for his services, was, at his age, to ride in the Companion Cavalry alongside Alexander in the dust of Gaugamela. It was such pleasure to be able to allow him this simple wish, and I'll always remember the day he came to me covered in dust after several charges and exclaimed with a schoolboy's enthusiasm, "Oliver, you know I've just done the *one* thing I wanted most of all to do in my entire life...I can never thank you enough." If only he knew what great pleasure he gave me. A straight runner, Mr. Fox.

He writes about the extraordinary details of film-making with an outsider's humorous view of another species, recalling Lillian Ross's dry observations on John Huston's "The Red Badge of Courage". It is very moving to see the admissions on Robin Lane Fox's part of the differences he has come to understand between his 1973 history and what may really have happened. I think historians, who have an open mind, would enjoy sharing these insights. Obviously, this leads to one of the most interesting theses of this book: What is this thing – history, myth, fact?

I am deeply touched by the author's open-mindedness, and honestly surprised by his intellectual humility. I think we all had to be humbled in some profound way to understand. Alexander deserves no less, as he too, requisite to his greatness, underwent some of the greatest humiliations of all. But, as his was not a complaining nature, these secrets shall remain forever locked in his big heart.

What was he like? As Colin Farrell says, "I'd give everything I have in this film to spend five real minutes with Alexander!"

I'd do the same, but barring that, I've spent three years with "him" now—and, difficult as it's been at times, I don't regret one moment of it. It's been a privilege, an honor beyond the ordinary. As Ptolemy says in the film, "In his presence, we were better than ourselves."

Oliver Stone
Paris, July 29, 2004

"Through Zeus, Alexander believed he was specially favoured by heaven: through Homer, he had chosen the ideal of a hero, and for Homer's heroes there could be no turning back from the demands of honour. He had the romantic's sharpness and cruel indifference to life: he was also a man of passionate ambitions who saw the intense adventure of the unknown. He did not believe in impossibility: man could do anything, and he nearly proved it."

Robin Lane Fox, Alexander The Great (1973)

"I concede that he did achieve unity – of a kind. I am reminded of the unforgettable final scene of Ingmar Bergman's film, The Seventh Seal, in which the disparate cast, their differences at last reconciled, float hand in hand over the horizon in the ethereal dance of death led by Death triumphant. That was the unity of Alexander – the whole of mankind, Greeks and Macedonians, Medes, Persians, Bactrians and Indians, locked together in a never-ending dance of death".

A.B. Bosworth, Alexander the Great and the Decline of Macedon, Journal of Hellenic Studies (1986) p.12

"He had a sense of mission, confirmed in him by religious rites and associations which were present from his youth onwards… His true claim to be Alexander the Great was that he did not crush or dismember his enemies, as the conquering Romans did – nor did he exploit, enslave or destroy the native people as the 'white men' have so often done, in America, Africa and Australasia – but he created, albeit only for a few years, a supra-national community capable of living internally at peace and of developing the concord and partnership which are so sadly lacking in the modern world."

Nicholas Hammond, Alexander The Great, King, Commander and Statesman (1980)

"L'illusion de la réalité n'a pas besoin de réalité."

Isabelle Brunetière (2003)

1. The View From the Ridge

Under the scorching September sun, Colin Farrell and three supporting filmstars steadied their horses on a hill-ridge in Morocco and prepared to look across the desert-valley which swept away in the distance. The four of them had ridden up to play Alexander the Great and his officers on the verge of the battle of Gaugamela which would change the course of history. Two thousand three hundred years ago, in late September 331 BC, Alexander and his officers had also ridden out on reconnaissance, looking out from just such a vantage-point at the massive army of the Persian King Darius with whom, on October 1st, they would engage their far smaller army in a battle for the mastery of Asia.

Unlike Alexander and his men, Farrell and his officers had only learned to ride their horses a month before. Like Alexander, they were not using stirrups, but unlike Alexander they had small leather saddles tucked beneath their horses' covering blankets. Like Alexander's men they had been prepared on a harsh routine of physical training but whereas Alexander's troops had trained for more than twenty five years, they had only been in a boot-camp for the past three weeks. Unlike Alexander's troops, they had been denied breakfast and women throughout. In silence, Colin and his guards had to size up the enemy's enormous numbers with a cool and confident gaze. However, it was particularly difficult to give one, because in the valley beyond them not a single tent or soldier was to be seen. Every one of the 200,000 enemy warriors was to be added later to the film-shot by 'visual effects' in the post-production phase.

For Colin, it was a first attempt at representing a character of history, let alone the greatest of all heroes from a distant ancient world. His heavy black horse, Bonze, was also a newcomer, having only been broken to the part of Alexander's Bucephalas since June. As Bonze played with the bit, the film-shot was to be one of Colin and his companions, shown in isolation on their hill. In real life, no shot is ever isolated. Dozens of crew-members busied round to realize it, running electric cables, focussing the cameras, announcing each take through a hand-held loud hailer and placing the specially-constructed camera-crane at an angle to the truck which had carted it up the steep hill-track. On a film-set, as shooting is prepared, everybody focuses on their own job. Up on the ridge there was one exception. In a short-sleeved, single-coloured shirt, with a soft grey hat tilted back on his head, stood the commanding presence of the film, its Director, Oliver Stone.

Four years had now gone by since Oliver last filmed outdoors on location. Each director has his own style and pattern, but the Stone style is famous for sudden improvisations on site. Would he move the entire shot round and redistribute his actors in a sequence as yet unspecified in his script? Many directors take the same shot a dozen times in a row without a clear view of which shot will be the valuable one in production. On his camera-monitor, Stone watches exactly what he is taking each time and when he knows he has taken what he wants, he is quick to move on, regardless of the number of possible shots left to him. The filming schedule for 'Alexander' would exploit this skill to the limit: ninety five days, whereas other epics of this scale are allowed about a hundred and twenty.

'Alexander: Day One, Take One, Scene One', the clapper-board announced: during every hour of filming for the next sixteen weeks, the script editor, Sue Field, would be standing at Oliver's side, noting down the points which have to be repeated to keep up continuity and writing down the camera-angles and the comments of Oliver on every single shot. On September 19th, the record began: "Sky-photo for Alexander. Point of view of Eagle [bird to be added later]. Static, then slow right to left drift…Track reveals Ptolemy and Hephaestion in B[ack] G[round]…Very good look from Alexander." "Next shot in sun with 2 actors looking up. Very good. Stutter on pan. Oliver liked a lot." "Next shot: Ptol[emy] looks up to Eagle with L[eft] H[and] up to shade eyes. Camera tracks to C[entre] S[creen] Hephaestion and Ptolemy. Their eye-line is to the Persian army. Cross from Right to Left on track. Good at start. N[ot] V[ery] G[ood] Ptolemy eyeline." From these comments, noted down on hundreds of shots in each of the days of shooting, the continuous epic is then cut and constructed.

What ever would Alexander the Great have made of it all? For nearly thirteen years, from 336 BC until his death on June 10th 323 BC, Alexander had been King of the Macedonians, leading them from their kingdom in northern Greece eastwards into Asia, through what is now Turkey, Syria, Egypt, Iraq and Iran, on into Afghanistan and north-western India. In three battles, he defeated armies of the Persian Empire, the ruling power in Asia. By the age of 25, he had become Pharaoh of Egypt, master of Babylon and many thousands of times richer than anyone in his Greek world. His aim was to reach the eastern edge of the world, bounded (he believed) by the Outer Ocean. In north-west India his troops would eventually refuse to go on, obliging him to return down the river Indus. He marched them through the south-east Iranian desert and eventually back to Babylon, bringing a chastened army to the site of his former welcome as a conqueror seven years before. But he was still only 32, the self-styled rival, and now the superior, of the heroes of the old Greek myths.

Alexander is the greatest conqueror and military genius in world history, the youthful overthrower of an Empire which had held down Asia for two hundred years. He has the spell of youth and the controversial fascination of a man of vast ambition who died without its aims being fully known. Was he only a conqueror and a killer, striving to master the world to the south and west after the hardships of India had denied him what he believed to be the boundary of the world in the East? Or did he also have a vision, an alarming one perhaps or an integrating one, of a world which he would then rule as its conqueror? And what, in his inner nature, drove him on to take such personal risks in hand-to-hand combat in the front line?

Alexander (Colin Farrell) reviews the Macedonian phalanx at Gaugamela.

Director Oliver Stone, Colin Farrell and the camera crew prepare a tracking shot 'on the ridge'.

Wounded Alexander (Colin Farrell) leaves the Indian battle on his Homeric Shield of Achilles.

Director Oliver Stone sets up a camera angle with photographic director Rodrigo Prieto.

His life has an epic sweep, and he himself was alive to the power of epic and drama. Homer's incomparable poem, the Iliad (the 'Tales of Troy'), was his constant companion and its scrolls were kept under his pillow (as the film's Roxane discovers). Homer's hero Achilles was his publicly-acknowledged role model. Before his first battle, Alexander went up to the ancient city of Troy, contrary to all the demands of military strategy at that moment. There, he ran naked with his beloved friend, Hephaestion, and put crowns on what were believed to be the tombs of the hero Achilles and his similar friend, Patroclus. From Troy Alexander took what was thought to be the ancient shield of legendary Achilles, like the one described so unforgettably by Homer in his poem. It would accompany Alexander on his march as far as India, just as its replica, designed in six weeks for the film, would support the wounded Colin Farrell when carried from battle against opposing Indians.

These gestures by Alexander have a dramatic ring to them, and like his later successors, Alexander brought a theatrical element to the style of being a king. He quickly became the subject of fiction and legend. People invented a text of his Will, collections of his letters to his mother or to Aristotle, his famous tutor, and stories of marvellous exploits which he never undertook. In Egypt, by the third century AD, they became part of history's best-selling fiction, the 'Romance of Alexander', which was to spread into dozens of languages, a medieval 'Lord of the Rings' during the next thousand years. It described an awesome Alexander who crossed the world in search of immortality and even tried to fly in a basket or explore the ocean-floor in a forerunner of the submarine. One version of this Romance became known in seventh-century Arabia, and so Alexander is mentioned with honour in the Muslim Koran. In its Sura 18, he is praised for his piety and his reception from God of a mastery over all the world: he travelled to the places where the sun rose and set and built a barricade to protect the world from invaders. As a result, Alexander has been a respected figure in art, poetry and legend in the Muslim world. In real life, nonetheless, Alexander also enjoyed and exploited drama for his own and his troops' entertainment. As far as India, he had plays put on to amuse his men and he himself sent for the scripts of the great classic playwrights of Athens's past. Every week, unlike many directors, Oliver Stone would arrange for showings of selected 'dailies', or uncut film-sequences, of his 'Alexander' to his actors and the members of his crew. Alexander would have loved to see 'dailies' of his march and exploits, although they would have been vetted, no doubt, before being shown to his men.

For thirty years and more, Hollywood directors have toyed with the ultimate epic, a film on Alexander the Great. In 2004, it came true, but as Colin Farrell and his guards trotted down from their ridge, completion still seemed a far-off mirage. For Oliver, it had been a carefully-chosen breaking-in, so as to go gently on his actors, but there was also the up-lifting sense of a dawn, an adventure with a new beginning. "Fortune favours the bold," he had written as the foreword to his filmscript, taking the words from the Roman poet Virgil's Aeneid. By the eighth shot on the ridge, there had been a sudden darkening in the sky behind, and then, a perfect rainbow spanning the view. It seemed a divine omen, like the missing eagle which was to be added to the shot. The gods, perhaps, were on the enterprise's side after all.

5

Olympias (Angelina Jolie) offers a tame snake to the frightened child Alexander (Jessie Kamm).

Pre-production image of the Lighthouse, one of the seven wonders of the world, to be seen from Ptolemy's balcony in Alexandria.

2. A Film Is Born

Film makers have long been fascinated by the idea of a big film on Alexander, but by 2001 three huge projects were being worked on simultaneously. The American television company, Home Box Office (HBO), was planning the most expensive of all, a series of ten one-hour episodes to be directed by Mel Gibson with a reputed budget of $200 million. There was talk of a film-epic by Martin Scorsese and there was a partnership between Dino di Laurentiis, now in his eighties, and Baz Luhrmann (Australian director of 'Moulin Rouge') who were seriously engaged on a script. Outsiders gave Oliver Stone only a one in three chance of being the director who first made the idea a reality.

Hollywood films about the ancient world have a history of using their subjects as a mirror in which to see contemporary American concerns. Oliver had already made films about the America of his adult lifetime, including the much discussed films about Kennedy and Nixon. Was he simply interested in Alexander, outsiders wondered, as a comment on the world's new disorder? Alexander had invaded and conquered the entire near East, from Egypt to what is now Afghanistan, including Iraq and Iran. On the way, he proclaimed 'liberation' and he restored democracies in the Greek cities on Asia's western coast. The liberation was a success, and it did not lead to local civil wars. Films about the past have a way of idealizing a distant ancient hero so as to show up the failings of modern politicians: would Stone's 'Alexander' take a similar line? In fact, the origins of Oliver's interest in the subject were older and subtler. At no point is his film a comment on what critics have described as 'Stone's USA', or on contemporary world events.

It was simply Alexander's story, the greatest story from the ancient world, that first appealed to Oliver, back in his days at New York University's Film School in 1969. The main outline of events in the story is known, but the motives, the characters, the tone of it all are lost or disputed. Where historians are obliged to guess, surely a film-maker, Oliver thought, could validly compose a drama? Yet very few dramatists have ever attempted it: there is nothing by Shakespeare and more recently, only a short-lived play in the early 1950's by Terence Rattigan in London. Historical novels have never really worked, either, although thousands of readers persisted with Mary Renault's sentimental trilogy in the 1970's. Somehow, the dialogue is unreadable in cold print. On film, the main precursor is Robert Rossen's unsatisfactory 'Alexander The Great', with Richard Burton in 1956. It ends early in Alexander's career, because the attempt to tell the whole story in a sequence proved impossible in only two hours. Burton adopts a hollow 'royal' style, like a debased Shakespearean King Henry. The studio also influenced the script. During America's

McCarthy purges of the 1950's, Rossen was one of those accused of 'communist' sympathies: he had a mental crisis when forced out by accusers. Initially, his script had dwelt on the murder of King Philip, Alexander's father, and alleged that Alexander had brought it about. The cinema version was obliged to be much more restrained.

At N.Y.U., Oliver also took a course in Greek mythology, following on from his (less successful) one in translated Greek classics at Yale. The Greek myths connected with Alexander's story and gave it a further dimension in his mind. But the story lay dormant in him until early summer 1989 when it was crystallized by an outline submission, sent to him 'on spec' by Munich-based producer, Thomas Schühly.

By then in his late thirties, Schühly had worked as a producer with the great German film-maker, Fassbinder. As a young boy, Thomas had listened to the ancient Greek myths and Homer's poems which were read to him in his educated south German household. As a Catholic schoolboy, he had learned Latin, and Alexander's story had always fascinated him. In translation, he knew the ancient sources for it, but he was never trained as a historian. At universities in Germany, he studied law and philosophy, including ancient philosophy. What he sent to Oliver was an unusual compound of abstract philosophy, historical insight, dramatic shaping and modern parallels.

Thomas did not know of Oliver's existing interest in Alexander, but he had chosen his man carefully. Oliver's Vietnam films, especially 'Platoon', qualified him to make a major battle movie: there had been an emotional intensity, Thomas felt, in his script-writing for 'Midnight Express' and 'Scarface' which could dramatise a person of Alexander's standing. In the 1980's, Schühly believed, there were only two directors who could pull it off: Coppola (already old) or Stone. When I eventually met Thomas, he had finished work on a film of the fantasising Baron von Munchausen. "Oliver", he told me, "has the skills of the painter Caravaggio", the Italian master of light and darkness, realism and focus, who had led a famously turbulent life, "he is Caravaggio and I am Munchausen; the result? The beginnings of 'Alexander'."

In his submission, Thomas insisted that an Alexander film must address the question of greatness. One side of it must be the greatness of Alexander the general and the man of battle, but there was also a greatness, however alarming, in Alexander's vision and horizon. What Thomas stressed was Alexander's reaction to the cultures of the world he conquered: he adopted bits of Persian royal style: he liked and promoted Iranians; was he, Thomas wondered, " the first 'politician' who had the idea of integrating the different cultures into one comprehensive whole?" (it seems a bit much, but the roots of this notion do lie way back in Germany with the historian Jacob Droysen's famous studies in the 1830's). If so, Alexander was at odds here with his famous teacher, Aristotle.

In the person of Aristotle, so Thomas wrote to Oliver, we can see a "guardian (a keeper of the Grail) of 'purebred' Greek culture exclusively of Greek make". "Alexander's curiosity, his tolerance, his inclination for the Orient and his idea to unite them must have caused horror and fear in Greece…" There are hints in the ancient sources that pupils of Aristotle hated Alexander and perhaps plotted to murder him. For Thomas, it was a 'safe assumption'. "Whenever purist-'ideologists' see their system and their power endangered

Setting up Alexander's victorious entry through the Babylon Gate with crowds and caged animals.

Pre-production drawing of the Persian-style decoration for walls of the Babylon palace.

A weary Alexander (Colin Farrell) works late at his desk out East.

– possibly through a 'charismatic' person – then the 'taking care' of the troublemaker is the accepted way of solving the problem". Why, Schühly wondered, do "personalities characterised by a super-human charisma so often meet a violent death – Socrates, Jesus, Martin Luther King: you name them!"

But there was much more to the story than this scope for a conspiracy-theory. Correctly, Thomas believed that "the big US productions describe the 'feeling of life' of a Greek always on the basis of protestant-American moral codes... This is absurd and (above all) boring... I am sure, we can ask more of the audience". The 'basis' for Alexander himself was the epic poetry of Homer and its ethics: it was 'the Bible to his Moses', and a film must be based on those ethics. It must also pose the question: was Alexander's campaign "worth it"? In Thomas's view, the result was a "wider culture, across the old barriers" but the questions (which he posed very well) about Alexander's darker side and all the suffering which his ambitions caused must also be posed on film. For Thomas, "Alexander mastered the art of winning the support of people he defeated" but he was not in the business of 'dreaming' or 'bringing 'Unesco' to the world'. He was brought up in a Macedonia which was more like the world of the Godfather. In 1973, I had written of Alexander's Macedon as "closer to the code of the mafia than to moralists removed in time". This remark in my history-book now gained an unexpected life.

The nineteenth-century German philosopher and classical scholar Friedrich Nietzsche was also central to Thomas' submission. "The human-being", Nietzsche wrote and Thomas quoted to Oliver, "carries within him a dreadful double-face. Perhaps these 'terrible talents' are a fertile soil which give rise to all humanity in our emotions and actions. This is why the Greeks, the most human of all peoples, reflect within their characters a trait of cruelty, of a desire for destruction, as does the tiger. That trait is visible in the exaggerated, almost grotesque reflection of Greece which is Alexander the Great. It is a trait which, throughout their history and their mythology, must scare us, because we confront it with the effeminate notion of modern humanism".

Maybe other directors in Hollywood have received packets of Nietzsche with submissions for an epic film. For Thomas, the 'tiger' in Alexander must never be lost among modern, post-Christian psychology. "Why did the army follow Alexander?", he asked me in Bangkok, years later, "Not so as to see the end of the world... It was 'animalesque': they follow the strong guy, the leading wolf in the wolf pack. They looked in the mirror, and saw something about themselves. They did not just follow youth... Read Nietzsche; read Kafka as he was walking in the zoo in Prague: he saw aspects of us men in the panthers in the cages. The animals remind us where we've come from..." For Thomas, Alexander's drama is a drama about beauty, not paranoia or increasing isolation. Alexander had the "beauty of a tiger, and so the gods were jealous. Achilles had it too, and he was fast. He was 'swift-footed Achilles'... Achilles had the glory of a 100-metre athlete." But Alexander had much more depth than his hero Achilles: "he had read books, he had heard Aristotle... he had a wider will to know..." Alexander did indeed read drama and history; he had Asia's roads measured and Asia's resources observed (German scholars have even seen him as the patron of 'scientific researches', with funding sent home to Aristotle). For

11

Thomas, this wider knowledge surely brought a questioning which 'swift-footed Achilles' never knew. In it lies Alexander's drama, as Thomas explained to Oliver in movie terms: Alexander "was born into a Godfather world… but then he 'married out', not to a Sicilian-Macedonian but to a distant girl from Bactria, Roxane… and then he questioned his childhood world while he lived on… the 'Godfather' becomes 'Lawrence of Arabia'. Alexander's own Iliad becomes an Odyssey in search of himself…"

Self-searching Alexander is not many sceptical scholars' view of him nowadays, but Thomas added a crucial point for Oliver's benefit. "It certainly didn't happen by chance that even the great dramatists kept their distance from 'overdimensional' personalities in history. There are only two successful examples here… 'Citizen Cane' and 'Amadeus'. To solve the problem of communication between the hero and the spectator, the authors introduced a third person – the 'mediator' – Joseph Cotton and Salieri, respectively". In Thomas' view, Alexander must be presented through a similar narrator-'mediator', a bridge between his complex personality and the audience. Only then could a film "answer the question 'what made Alexander run?'" His own suggestion was to choose the son of one of the Iranian families who were incorporated by Alexander or the son of a marriage between a Macedonian soldier and an Oriental. These people were called the 'New Generation' or 'Successors' (Epigonoi) by Alexander, but nothing more is known of them. Suppose (Thomas suggested) we were to follow one of them from Alexander's death, ten, fifteen years later, a puzzled 'Epigonos' (Successor) who wants to know what his 'founder-father' Alexander was really like. He could go round the survivors and talk with them and bit by bit, learn the dreadful answer: that Aristotle and his pupils had had the great Alexander poisoned.

There was force, certainly, in this idea, but first 'Caravaggio' had to reply. On June 11, 1989, Oliver responded: "Brilliant analysis". "Enemy as Greeks, not just Persians. Concept of a culture propagated by Alexander against the localisation of pure Greek thinking: a brilliant theme for a character study. Comparison to Lawrence made me understand, and at the same time excited me as never before… Ah, yes Thomas: you have created in my eyes at last the true hero. I understand. Bless you… you are truly a great producer!!" From this response, 'Alexander's' slow birth began. But first, "let me make my smaller pictures, maybe two, maybe three, urgent, smaller political pictures" (they ended up as the vast 'JFK' and 'Nixon'). There was also talk of Oliver directing a film of Cortes, but, he said, it did not really interest him. "I will learn from them, and at last be ready for the great masterpiece of my life… In Alexander, I have found, as you have pointed out, 'intolerance' (in Aristotle, in Alexander's older officers, in some of the Greeks) upon which to climb up the heights of a life".

Surveying Oliver Stone's work, I now realise how much was already in the Alexander story for him. There was his frequent theme of battle and fading idealism ('Platoon'; 'Born on the Fourth of July'). In Macedonia, Alexander saw open quarrels between his mother and his father Philip and the topic of his father's achievements became a difficult one for him in later life: compare 'Heaven and Earth' or 'Nixon' or 'Scarface'. In Alexander's story, there is a strong sense of the 'beast' within us, especially when Cleitus is murdered: compare, of course, 'Platoon'. In Schühly's view, there is also a hero who questions his previous self: compare 'Born on the Fourth of July'. Might Oliver even show Alexander through the eyes of the peoples he invaded, like his 'Heaven and Earth' on Vietnam? There was even a historic meeting between Alexander and some Indian wise men: compare the Indian shaman who is grafted into 'Natural Born Killers' and 'U-Turn'. Above all, there was Alexander's awareness of the god Dionysus, his 'discovery' of Dionysus's deeds in India and his readiness to attribute disasters to the god Dionysus's anger.

In Oliver's film 'The Doors' (1990), Dionysus is present in pop-star James Morrison's story of excess and decline: Dionysus's image is even shown in the film. A year earlier, Thomas Schühly's submission had brought Dionysus back to Oliver's notice and had quoted the young Nietzsche, whose views of the god's role is so famous. In Nietzsche's view, Greek civilisation had evolved through a tension between the gods Apollo and Dionysus. Apollo had represented 'measure' and 'boundaries'. Dionysus (Nietzsche believed) was a later invader in the Greek Olympian gods' kingdom. His power was to break down the barriers between individual elements and to induce a state of 'intoxication' and utter 'self-forgetting'. In interviews, given in 2000, Oliver drew on this imaginative contrast between Apollo and Dionysus, which appealed to his own view of the the world. For Nietzsche, Dionysus was the cause of a "blissful ecstasy" in a "tumultuous wild chase across all the scales of the soul under the influence of narcotic stimulants or… at the approach of spring when the whole of action is pervaded by the lust for life". In Greece, the essence of Dionysus (he believed) was felt in music, one of Oliver's great loves, on which Apollo had been imposing a sober rhythm. "It was for me", Thomas Schühly told me, "to be the Apollo to Oliver's Dionysus…" Eventually, in the filming, narrator-mediator Ptolemy (Anthony Hopkins) would pause near the end between their two statues, Apollo and Dionysus. In Greece, Dionysus had been tamed by his duet with his fellow-god. Out in the East, however, a wilder Dionysus had persisted (Nietzsche imagined) in an "excess of general indiscipline" and a "repulsive return of sensuality and cruelty". It had been worst of all in Babylon " where human beings regressed to the condition of tigers and monkeys". In the script Thomas always disliked 'steamy' Babylon, as opposed to the 'purity' of the deserts or the rational planning of the new Alexandria. But Alexander had 'liberated' Babylon, and then returned to die there. Babylon was to be increasingly central to Oliver's thinking, and in November and December 2003, Babylon was to be staged, away from the 'approach of spring', in a freezing cold studio at London's Pinewood.

Schühly cherished one more idea: Gore Vidal should serve as the project's artistic consultant. Like many, he respected Vidal's fictional life of the Roman emperor Julian (which historians of the period dismiss) and Vidal's novel Creation in which the Persian king Xerxes and wise men of varying ages meet in a brothel in Babylon. By Spring 1990, Thomas had equipped Oliver with nearly 250 pages of 'Producer's Specifications' in which extracts from the ancient sources kept company with quotations from Mary Renault, comments by Napoleon, Nietzsche and German history books. In their discussions, Thomas would also urge Oliver to read the novel about Alexander by Thomas Mann's son, Klaus. It emphasised the fear of death and Alexander's need to overcome it (the road to true freedom): a trace of it survives in the film's Indian battle scene. At the end, however, an angel appears to Alexander and invites him to return to earth and try to repeat his deeds, but this time without a sword. Why were the up-to-date arguments of Alexander-scholars not given more prominence? In Thomas's view, they, too, are subjective and at this early stage, too much historical debate would smother the project. "Oliver should aim for 'his' Alexander because there is no such thing now as 'the' Alexander. Goethe is right... 'when a man is dead, we should leave him to the poets'". Oliver must claim the poetic licence of Shakespeare. "Think of Macbeth", he told him, "not Hamlet: Hamlet agonizes as the first bourgeois man, but Alexander creates his own destiny" (actually, Stone's favourite Shakespearean play is Richard III).

In Summer 1990, the two of them travelled to Italy. In Rome, Thomas introduced his new ally to Fellini ("Big Hollywood, Mr Stone... Big Hollywood...") and then in Ravello, to Gore Vidal. There was so much to discuss, Greek ethics, Babylon, sexual morality, Alexander's aims, and the meeting became highly convivial. But it was not a meeting of minds and Schühly knew that neither would work with the other. For the moment Stone was too busy with his cluster of 'smaller' films. In 'Natural Born Killers' (1994), the 'new Dionysus' then gave free rein to excess and 'intoxication': only afterwards was he ready for an Alexander script. He began to sort his own notes; he turned to American Greek scriptwriter Laeta Kalogridis and set her to work with him to produce a first draft. By spring 1996 elements were beginning to form: the second draft began with a silent scene of Alexander's death, a flying signet-ring and a journey back to Macedon with Ptolemy writing there as a narrator. From then on, however, the story became historically all over the place. The Persians actually started by invading Macedon and Hephaestion first met Alexander on the way to fight them. Worse, Alexander married Roxane in Sogdia before fighting a decisive battle against Darius in Syria and that battle was Issus (333BC), not Gaugamela (331BC). The scenes in India were hurried, and they included, quite wrongly, Hephaestion's death.

'Dramatic licence' is all very well, but Alexander is a historical figure and just because he died sixty generations ago, we cannot turn the known events of his life upside down. As a historian this entire draft strikes me as misdirected effort: without a historian, how could the story ever stay straight and how could the resulting 'Alexander' have any of the structure which shaped the real Alexander? Too many 'history' epics have recently been filmed with this disregard for known facts. But it was only a draft, and soon there was a change of direction.

By late 1996, Oliver was working with Andy Vajna (the producer of 'Nixon') and discussing the project with Mario Kassar (producer of 'The Doors') and Arnon Milchan (the producer of 'JFK' and 'Natural Born Killers'). Schühly was still pursuing the subject too and the rights to it were becoming more complicated. Meanwhile, Vajna's company faced financial difficulties.

In the small world of Hollywood, ideas are never secret. Inevitably, there were rival 'Alexanders' in the wind, rumours about Ridley Scott, rumours about Scorsese and a real attempt which was gaining strength behind Dino di Laurentiis, a figure in Stone's past

(Oliver had written the script for him on 'Year of the Dragon'). While Oliver's 'U-Turn' (1997) and 'Any Given Sunday' (1999) took priority, his Alexander project ran the risk of running out of time. Even in 1999, when Oliver was free again, Thomas Schühly remembers how the two of them discussed a possible film on Homer's Iliad instead: the 'easier' prelude, he felt, would be Troy. He recalls reading to Oliver passages from Robert Fagles' English translation of Homer. "Tell me a story…", Oliver would ask him, casting round for a point in the narrative on which to distribute the emphasis.

In Spring 2000 the project took a decisive turn: it found its studio and leading financier. Oliver had known Moritz Borman for more than twenty years: they had also worked on a project on the Mexican revolution. When Moritz asked him, "What next?", Oliver replied, "Alexander". Moritz had recently floated the publicly-quoted International Media AG in Germany and the success of the 'Terminator' films had increased his financial strength. Back in Germany he was also connected with a group of private investors, IMF. Even the draft 'Alexander' scripts attracted the IMF investors' interest, encouraged by producer Matthias Deyle, with whom Schühly also had close relations. What was needed was pre-production funding, to pay for script work, location hunting and so forth. With the IMF investors' support, Moritz arranged for its commitment.

Like Schühly, Moritz Borman had also studied Latin as a schoolboy in Germany. He knew Alexander's importance, but with a smile, he recalls how he encouraged Oliver not to be too tied to history. In discussions, Moritz continued to insist on the need for a unifying drama, for practical appeal to an audience, for a sense of fun and 'triumph', however Oliver chose to pull Alexander's dynamism together. In June 2000, Schühly was still arguing the need for a 'narrator-mediator': "I see the point," Oliver replied, "of seeing Alexander through other eyes and I would be glad to explore it. Certainly the Oriental point of view would be fascinating…" but Mary Renault had already done it. Moreover, his 'Nixon' had worked without a "voice-over in that insanely paranoid White House… and yet… somehow my instinct tells me it can't be done from inside, by putting ourselves in the sandals of Alexander." A key dimension of the film was forming, the use of a narrator. At the same time, "I want to explore the differences, through Alexander's eyes, between three exotic philosophies / religions – the Babylonian priests, Hindu priests and Egyptian priests at Siwah – and his own Greek one". It is an area where films can go badly wrong, but Schühly was willing to try, sending notes on the nature of the soul or Greek views on love: "please let me know if you are still interested in this topic?"

First, Oliver wanted a draft from an interim script-writer: Moritz suggested he use Chris Kyle, known to him for his work on 'K19'. Kyle had no prior knowledge of the Greeks or the history, but Oliver had handwritten versions of his own script as well as copies of Laeta Kalogridis's work. So he took his 1996 draft and set Kyle to work anew. In late 2001, Schühly sent in an essay on 'greatness' for the new script, fearing it might be lost: "greatness of soul must renounce personal gain for the sake of morality… All is complete if a grace of character and defiance of death are added… the will to win and to reconcile… and always with a grain of gentleness and kindness…" But also, "A power was never founded without crime… this is complemented by the indisputable relation of the genius with mania... p.s. We spoke about the cast for Philip... the only actor disposing of such physical and kingly presence is Sean Connery."

In reply, Oliver found the views on greatness (but not Connery) 'very helpful', but "be generous and do not forget to let go some of your 'darlings' in regard to Alexander... I am moved by the amount of faith you have in me, although I am not sure I can live up to it..." But: "we should seriously prep this movie, starting as early as March..." (2002). The 'trinity' were working to the same end: Moritz emphasised Alexander's youth, the drama of his parents, the need to carry the audience along with a pre-Christian world, while Schühly insisted on specific Greek ways of thinking and Greek morality, at times at an abstract level (Plato is not a 'typical' Greek). In the centre was Oliver, aware of both and knowing that he would not make a simple 'action movie', as if it would be 'enough' for a supposedly dumbed-down audience. "Fassbinder had certainty...", Thomas later told me, "but Oliver has certainty only as a director: as a writer, he explores, he works in metaphors". As for his search for 'wisdom', "basically, he's still a Catholic Christian, although he doesn't accept it... Guilt, obsession, what have they to do with 'consumer Buddhism'? Dionysus is not the Pope..."

Film-scripts die as easily as horses in Alexander's army and even with Moritz's commitment, the project was only one of three on the streets. Oliver had plans for a love story to be set around international medical workers, 'Beyond Borders' (significantly, with Angelina Jolie): he was considering the story of a prisoner of war, Billy Garwood, who had gone over to Vietnamese culture and stayed with it in preference to America (the disaster of 9/11 then killed off any hope of that film being made). There were also his plans for documentaries: on Castro, on Arafat. By winter 2001, Di Laurentiis was pressing hard: he had a director (Baz Luhrmann), studio support (Universal; DreamWorks) and in principle an Alexander (Di Caprio), but did he really have a script? Chris Kyle's drafts appeared, and Schühly's comments on them were penetrating. "Where is Alexander's attested keenness for knowledge and new discoveries?" (Alexander's 'keenness' reached some strange conclusions, but it certainly needed to come in...) What about the Macedonians' own experience? "We are dealing with a gang of simple Macedonian soldiers that within a few years, experienced impressions we can almost compare to a space-odyssey. Egypt, Babylon, Persia, India". Inevitably, the dialogue was still missing a 'royal tone' for Alexander: why not draw more on Homer? Meanwhile the scripts for the HBO television project were going down exactly the opposite route: foul language, and an Alexander who sounded like a gangster from the Bronx with plenty of homosexual insults between the troops.

Above all, Thomas urged, "I find it deplorable we have now lost Aristotle...": in modern, minimalist scholarship there are historians who have lost him too, as if Alexander learned nothing from the world's greatest thinker. And what about Roxane? "Alexander's very intense reaction to this girl I would put in a kind of analogue to the love affair of Achilles and the queen of the Amazons. I always imagine Roxane as a kind of 'Indian-Amazon', taller than Alexander, of archaic elegance and noblesse. I certainly do not see an analogy to his mother... such a resemblance for Alexander would have led him to impotence..." But Oliver did not agree, and in his film, Roxane and Alexander's mother Olympias do stand in a crucial inter-relation. The "encounters of Alexander with Buddhism and Zoroaster are only on the level of pious calendar notes. Why is there no scene with the philosopher Diogenes, naked in his tub?" (Thomas always had Marlon Brando in mind for playing the famous cynic). "Surely they talked comprehensively?" Couldn't Philip and Olympias meet at the mysteries on the island of Samothrace and Alexander be conceived among sex, drugs and music? For, Alexander liked music, and "at Troy, he was not looking for the sword of his idol Achilles... but for his lyra!"

Oliver wondered if Chris could possibly take all this criticism, and anyway it was late. "There are times, Thomas, I wish you would pop up more promptly in the classroom than a generation later..." But the ideas were valid: please bring scripts of them, and yes, "Roxane is the weakest character, and we need any help or ideas". Her major presence in the film was now emerging: were there any documents on her? Someone had "strongly suggested that we use documents from the Vatican library which is in your backyard. He says these documents on Alexander are incomparable". (Actually, the texts there are not 'documents', and they are no help nowadays). And "lastly, Thomas, who is Lyra??" - as if Thomas's word for the Greek 'lyre' was one more mistress waiting to be described.

When Chris Kyle's final draft appeared, it went to and fro between key points in Alexander's career. The Indian battle came first in the film, and from the middle onwards Alexander's disastrous march through the Gedrosian desert became a repeated scene. The dialogue was still short and flat, and the price of including more major scenes was that the script lacked a total vision. It was valuable, not least for showing up new problems, but once again Oliver himself must now do his own script. Chris, however, had put in one ominous stage-direction. At the entry to the Gedrosian desert, "cages roll past carrying a variety of wild beasts, everything from tigers to monkeys... in the last cage, three historians sit at writing-desks, busily scribbling on parchments..." In preparation for the 'final push', Thomas recognised that he must now look beyond the tiger-cage. It was time to send for a historian from the human zoo.

Wall 'mosaic' of Alexander and Craterus's lion hunt from Ptolemy's study, modelled on a real mosaic from Pella.

Alexander (Colin Farrell) hits Cassander (Jonathan Rhys Meyers) against the wall of the Bactrian Council Chamber.

Alexander (Colin Farrell) angrily harangues his unwilling troops in India, watched by Craterus (Rory McCann) and Perdiccas (Neil Jackson).

3. When Robin Met Oliver

My introduction to 'Alexander' came in March, 2002 in the last week of the Oxford University term. I was teaching that earth-shattering topic, the strategy of the Spartans in the year 407BC, when the telephone rang and I made my acquaintance with Thomas Schühly. "Oliver Stone is making a film on Alexander the Great and I want you to go and meet him when he comes into London in a fortnight's time. I am most concerned that the script should be true to Alexander's greatness. You can talk to him about Homer, about Achilles, but it is Nietzsche who understood: Alexander was a fierce and beautiful tiger. We need you to talk with Oliver, to explain that the Macedonians were not Hollywood, not California. They did not spend all day with their therapists: Socrates dined on a couch, he did not psycho-analyse on one". Thomas was already in fine form: "Who is backing this film?", I asked him cautiously. "All of us", he assured me, "the money we now have comes from here in Germany. You are the historian, you can help Oliver hit the target. Maybe he will talk with you for an hour, maybe two hours - or maybe only twenty minutes. You'll enjoy it…". Greatness, Germany, tigers: was this film some sort of historical throw-back? "Good, good," Thomas had decided, "you'll go, and then we will make Alexander the *Greatest*". My two pupils were sitting in polite bafflement on the sofa, waiting to discuss whether a Spartan treaty with Persia in 407BC existed or not. Big game in the human jungle seemed very far away.

Oliver, in filming mode, does not observe holidays: we fixed to meet in his hotel in London's Covent Garden on Good Friday, 2002. I knew next to nothing about him, except that Thomas Schühly sounded excited, anxious and fond of him, in equal measure. He was famous, I did know, for Vietnam movies; he had fought there, I remembered; he had caused a stir with a film about JFK and of course, he was attacked for manipulating history. Manipulating historians, I reflected, would be more difficult.

It would be difficult because I had lived through so many of these film-overtures in the past thirty years. They began when my book on Alexander first came out, with an invitation to meet Gregory Peck in London's Ritz hotel in 1974. Dressed in the famous white suit, he told me his plans for an Alexander movie: Twentieth Century Fox would back it and he would play King Philip, the founding-hero, the man who really knew how it had all begun. Sadly, the project did not survive, but three years later Alexander's spell fell on Time Life instead. In autumn 1977, they embarked on what was to be a big docurama series on Alexander, supported by Greek sponsorship. The project set out with plans for an illustrated version of my book and a director whose most recent production was a film about prisons in the American South. Then, in autumn 1977, the Greek archaeologist Manolis Andronicos made his remarkable discoveries in the great burial mound at Vergina in Macedonia and uncovered a royal double tomb which he suggested cautiously to be King Philip's own. Subsequent study has confirmed this view, although outsiders tried to reject it: the Time Life project thus gained a third leg, an exhibition of the superb objects in the tomb of Alexander's father, to be seen in America's major museums and entitled The Search for Alexander, after a phrase in my book.

It was as well that the project had three legs, because one of them soon went lame. In 1978, the film-makers came over to Oxford for a winter meeting in the Randolph hotel: astrakhan coats and velvet collars were in evidence: so were female 'researchers', cigars and a detestation of cold English evenings. The hotel added to the atmosphere by serving fried potatoes which amazed the American guests by being green. We discussed locations: Iran was still an open country and so was Afghanistan, but the director was much more interested in what drugs were taken by Alexander and his officers and in an episode in which Alexander would enter Jerusalem and meet the High Priest of the Jews. There is not a shred of evidence that Alexander took any recreational drugs, except wine, and the tale of his meeting with the Jewish High Priest is a total fiction which began about 150 years after Alexander's death. The main technique of the film was to be the use of statues which would appear to speak. We took a friendly, but cautious, leave of one another and the next message I received was that the 'researcher' had now photographed all the ancient statues in Rome and Florence, none of which had anything to do with Alexander, and the team had reached Naples: should they go any further East, the cable asked?

When the script arrived in 1979, the Greek sponsors were understandably upset: it was the sort of text which begins with comments about the 'sickness of slavery poisoning Greece' and illustrates it by 'cut to scenes on the Parthenon frieze', the supreme icon of classical Athenian art which shows not a single slave in its famous procession. While visiting the publishers in New York in January 1980, I arranged to meet with John, the head of Time Films, and to plead for scrapping the entire script and starting again. I found him in his office on the phone to Jane Fonda's agent, insisting that she could not have another hairdresser in her trailer where she was sulking out on set. He listened carefully to me, and over lunch the next day, told me that he would scrap the entire team, hand the film over to David Selznick (whom I had never heard of), tell him to work directly with me and give me a right of veto. It would have been a dream arrangement for a historian, but first, he told me, "heads will have to roll". I returned to Oxford for a new term, alarmed that I would be completely out of my depth with a film-maker. After a week, I rang Time Films to discover that heads had indeed rolled: they had sacked John before he could sack anyone else. The project had already lost millions of dollars without anything being filmed. It was now to be scaled back to a cheaply-filmed documentary in which James Mason narrated a needlessly unimaginative script by the English novelist Simon Raven. I never even watched it.

No sooner had Time Life lost millions than Steven Spielberg entered the arena. In the early 1980's copies of my book were scattered round his company offices, Amblin' Productions; he became caught up with the idea of a massive 'Alexander' movie; I heard the news from a long-standing friend who had moved from Chelsea to California and befriended a Spielberg associate called Menno. On the phone to me Menno was enthusiastic: "Steven really gets the youth side of history: this guy Alexander was twenty five, and he conquered the world: how did he dream it up?" It sounded to me as if we might film young Alexander dreaming in a pony paddock at the base of Beverly Hills, like Judy Garland in the Wizard of Oz. Options on my book, a draft outline and a research plan brought a note of reality, but four months later, I was informed the project was over: Steven had 'decided to get out of youth'. So he made 'Colour Purple' instead.

By the early 1990's, when Oliver was said to be interested, I had come to believe that the project was under an ancient Greek curse. In 1996, during his collaboration with Andy Vajna, Andy's Cinergi Entertainment did take another twelve-month option on my book (with the improbable promise of a share of the box-office net profits): nothing further happened, and Cinergi failed to raise funding. So in 2002 it might be Easter, Alexander might be a 'beautiful tiger', but after one more run round the stadium, I assumed it would all be left to sleep in peace.

Waiting for Oliver outside his hotel suite, I had the impression of smiling blonde ladies going to and fro in knee-length boots and a steady, polite male presence, wearing black rimmed spectacles and knowing when to say the minimum. I never imagined that for two years, this courteous young assistant, Rob Wilson, would be my constant link with Oliver, patiently accepting my inability to master e-mails but sharing my love for Lubisch's film Ninotchka (1939), starring Garbo. When Oliver appeared, I had not expected such a burly presence. "I'm a war-veteran", I later found that Oliver had written of himself, "I stand six feet tall, have very black hair, eyes and brows, and some think I can be very intimidating looking. If I were five foot five and looked like Woody Allen, I don't think people would think me such a threat." There was also a thin 'Oriental' moustache and an immediate attempt at casting me. "God, you've got long arms," he said in a flash, which is, in fact, true: "where did you get them from?" "Over the centuries," I replied, and he laughed. "You Brits, you think you've always existed: you look like Ian Fleming. Let's go in."

We sat opposite each other at a low table, and Oliver explained his needs with a marked copy of my Alexander book in his hand. He was making an Alexander film; he had worked with script-writers on several drafts, but he did not feel the script was right yet and as he usually did, he would take it over and write it all again himself. He himself was unsure: he did not know if he could ever measure up to the challenge. So: I was Alexander's historian, how would I do it? There was nothing for it but to plunge in.

I talked of how I would look at Alexander through various characters' eyes: people loved him, people hated him, as they still do. I would see him through the eyes of his first mistress, the Persian noblewoman Barsine, who was much older than Alexander. She had known him as a little boy and had never expected to be captured with the spoils in Asia and eventually to become mother of his illegitimate son (or so she said). I would see him through his personal publicist Callisthenes, kinsman of Aristotle, who left his researches into ancient history (had I now left mine?) and set out as the historian celebrating 'Alexander's Deeds'. Seven years later, he became disenchanted and Alexander had him put to death. I would then change focus to his secretary, the able Greek Eumenes: he might have helped to fake a text of Alexander's 'last plans' and to issue the so-called 'Diaries' of Alexander's last days in Babylon. Finally, I would switch to Thais, who had begun her life as an Athenian courtesan. She is said to have encouraged Alexander and his men to burn down the vast Persian palace at Persepolis during a spectacular drinking-party. She then lived with Ptolemy in Egypt to whom she bore three children: what memories they must have had.

"You will have emptied the cinema in seven minutes flat", Oliver concluded, "But it's all so vivid to you; why?" So I tried to explain how I had lived with these images in my head for forty years now, how I always try to visualise what ancient texts, our only evidence, describe so briefly and try to see it in my mind's eye, like an inner sort of film. Alexander sometimes did dreadful things, but he had the fascination of youth and the errors of impulsive extravagance. His men adored him, and we need to understand why, whatever we think now about conquerors who kill thousands of people because they refuse to surrender to them. Alexander measured himself against the heroes of myth; he believed he was the begotten son of Zeus and he lived out a rivalry with the Achilles of Homer. What had been his aims: ever more conquest, simply because he was addicted to it (he has been studied for symptoms of 'traumatic stress disorder', like modern war-veterans) or a vast new kingdom, Alexander's kingdom, whose people would serve him regardless of their ethnic origin?

"OK, let's begin again: I'm going to have one narrator who can choose from the story which he witnessed. I've chosen Ptolemy: what do you think?" "Excellent: he is the obvious choice, and Ptolemy actually wrote a history of the Alexander he had known." "So - tell me about Ptolemy in Alexander's lifetime." So I talked of their friendship, of Ptolemy's own heroic combats during Alexander's expedition, of his ability to be 'economical with the truth' in his subsequent history and of his acceptance of the miraculous. "Alexander went off with a small group of companions to the desert-oracle at Siwah, and Ptolemy claimed that they were escorted by talking snakes, the whole way there and the whole way back". "Talking snakes?", Oliver interrupted, "do you expect the audience to believe that? We're not making a Disney film about Alexander's horse: how old was Ptolemy?" "Well, he lived until the late 280's, and some people think he was born after Alexander." "Was he or not?" "I doubt it: we don't know." "Was he Philip's son by one of his mistresses?" "That's probably a later story, to connect him to the royal house." It is a rare story and I had not expected Oliver to know it. "Is it wrong?" "Probably." "But it's not wrong that he should be old at the end of his life?" "No: he would be at least 75." "When did he write his history?" "When he was old, in my view: in the 290's or 280's." "OK, then he's very old." Months later, Anthony Hopkins' make-up would reflect this discussion.

So, Oliver resumed, "take me through the details. Ptolemy is going to be remembering Alexander: is he writing it all down?" "No, he is dictating" (I was guessing...) "Dictating to whom?" "A slave". "On which side is the slave?" "I don't know: let's say, on his left." "And what is the slave called: Scylax? I like that name." "No, Scylax was a sea-captain:

Old King Ptolemy (Anthony Hopkins) reminisces on his balcony in Alexandria with Cadmus (David Bedella) behind him.

Alexander (Colin Farrell) marries Roxane (Rosario Dawson) in Bactria and declares harmony between the two peoples.

Alexander's army marches on the Hindu Kush mountains towards India.

Alexander's father King Philip (Val Kilmer), one-eyed as in history.

call him Cadmus, that would be neat." "Why?" "Cadmus was the legendary introducer of the alphabet into Greece from Phoenicia, the Levant. So the slave can be a Levantine, a second Cadmus writing for Ptolemy". "OK, OK - Cadmus. And is Cadmus standing up or sitting down?" "Both," I said, guessing frantically. "But if he's standing, how is he writing? And what is he writing on?" "On a waxed tablet perhaps - no, on a roll of papyrus with a reed pen." "How does Ptolemy speak to him?" "Without restraint, as if he is completely loyal or even irrelevant, as a slave, a non-person - and sometimes Ptolemy is rough with him. He hits him once, perhaps." "Are you sure?" "No."

Out of this rapid fire, Cadmus was born and his scenes with Ptolemy originated. I was to become used to these barrages, answers to which were frantically copied down long-hand on a writing-pad by Oliver who shared my distaste for a laptop. After this salvo, Oliver stopped: "you're hesitating too often: you're guessing, aren't you? But I can't. I have to make a movie. I have to see it in my mind first, right down to the details. Let's go back to where you started. Tell me about his historian Callisthenes" - so I did - "and tell me how they burnt down Persepolis" - so I did, with gusto. "Were you there?" Oliver asked. "Sort of - but no." "Well, you make it seem like you were. But how am I going to cover all this action? There's thirteen years of it; I've too much already, and you've just added Persepolis. Do you realise - we have two and a half hours, maybe three. I'm going to have to leave out so many events. Every time we have a new location - you must accept this - it's going to cost us millions. So we can't do it all - can you live with that? That's one modern reason why Ptolemy has to be selective in what he tells." Then he paused. "Why are you prepared to talk to me like this?"

From a supposedly big ego, this question was one I had not expected. "Because you start by accepting that there is a challenge," I answered, "greater than both of us - that challenge is Alexander - to which we have to measure up. Because you have had a wider education and a wider life than the other Hollywood film-makers." "How do you mean?" What I meant was that I knew Oliver's mother was French; he knew Paris well; he had been at major American universities. And unlike me, he had fought in a horrible war and known real fear and ferocity. The result, I ventured, is that "you can accept that Alexander and his world are so much more varied and interesting than your own imagination. You won't turn him into a frustrated American movie-star or a Californian caught between his astrologer and his boyfriends." I told him how Spielberg had seemed to be mainly interested in Alexander's youth, but I did not think this youth was spent as a kid on a ranch, how George Lucas (another interested party in Alexander) was a technical expert but no historian. "It's your film, but if you want, it is for me to tell you the framework. There are things that we simply know - 'history' isn't all subjective - and you must know them. If you go against them, you have to know that you are going against them, and you must have good reasons - not just your own ego - for doing so. Think of Alexander's history as a half-finished building which has all the beams and girders in place, but all the gaps unfilled. You can then imagine how to fill the gaps in; with luck, your imagination will be different to Spielberg's or Lucas's. They do not read ancient history, they've seen nothing much about it; in my view, they would make a film about themselves or their impressions of America."

There was a grunt. "If I get you flown out to LA, would you come next weekend for a picnic up in the hills? It's a nice picnic up in the pine trees, and I'll ask my friends Lucas and Spielberg to come too and you can meet with them again (I'd explained my previous film-history, from Peck onwards) - and then you can tell them what you've just said. You should come - are you free?" "No, it's my busy time in the garden." "You prefer *gardening* to a picnic with these people? You're mad. They'd have to laugh." So we returned to the notepads. What were Alexander's dying words - the film could begin there? I told him of the late Mary Renault's guess, which she had once sent to me on a postcard - perhaps Alexander began to say "Krat-", and his officers quickly smothered him. He meant to say "To Krateros" (in Greek, 'Krateroi') but the jealous officers stopped him and then spread the word that he had been about to say "To the strongest" (in Greek 'Krat-istoi'). "Was she serious?" "Half," I said. And hints of it ended up in the script.

Ceaselessly I was battered with questions about Babylon (which I could not answer) and about the state of Greece in the 330's BC. "I need some details: change down a gear here. What games did the Greeks play at parties?" "The most famous is a game called kottabos, where the reclining guests would flick drops of wine at a cup balanced on a pole, often on a wall. If you hit the cup, you had to declare 'X' or 'Y is beautiful', naming your male crush of the moment". The Director was disbelieving: "what is this game of yours - some sort of Eton College fraternity rite?" So I called for wine-glasses, which were located discreetly by Rob in the adjoining kitchen and I explained how Greek cups had a 'stem' which you could hold in your hand while swirling the cup so as to mix the water and wine together (Greeks drank watered-down wine). With a triumphant flick, I then hit a picture on the hotel wall, and exclaimed 'Oliver is beautiful'. Oliver did not miss the game's potential. Two years later, the guests in the background of the partying at Pella would duly be playing kottabos on screen, while aiming at a cup fixed by magnets. "How did Greeks curse?", my kottabos-companion asked, "How did they swear?" This question is not easy to answer. "'To the crows', they would say". "We can't", Oliver retorted, "it doesn't sound credible. Find something else." So now I was taking notes too.

"What about Persian ceremonies: did the princesses dine with the men?" This question is not so easy, either. "What about their custom of bowing down, proskynēsis, is that how you pronounce it?" "Yes", and so I described this Persian social practice, a kiss on the face for social equals, a kiss blown by a particular gesture (I made it) from respectable visitors, and then the falling down and grovelling by social inferiors. "Would you grovel before William Tarn?" Oliver startled me by asking, for Sir William Tarn was the most idealising historian of Alexander between the 1920's and the 1950's and he is one whom I and others consider to be very mistaken. "No". "Why not - why are you historians so down on Tarn? He had generosity of spirit." So we discussed the polarised views which historians have taken of Alexander since Tarn and why, when the evidence is often against them. Oliver knew the debates, but on the matter of Persian kissing, he was unsure. "An audience won't follow it: most of them aren't monarchists, unlike you Brits." "I'm not". "Well, your audiences are."

We discussed why Alexander interested him and Oliver told me how far the story went back in his life, to N.Y.U., Yale and earlier to his reading as a young man. "Hephaestion is beautiful…" he said, looking at the half-empty wine-glass, "do you think Alexander ever said that? What about sex? Whatever we do, some people will try to say we're wrong here: Alexander wasn't a one-way 'gay', but he had intense male relationships." "Yes: from November 333, when he was 23 he had the Persian lady Barsine (who became pregnant), then a wife with whom he fell in love, then two more wives (probably political). But he had an intense erotic friendship too with Hephaestion, with whom he had grown up, and he had another lover, a Persian eunuch. So, there are ancient texts which simply assume he had sex with a male too." "But not only with males, and it wasn't unusual at his age. Did they have sex at those Etonian fraternity rites?" As an Etonian myself, I would have to say that some Etonians did, but never the ones whom you ask: in Alexander's world, I suggested that the idea of a 'homosexual nature' was not fully formulated, that sex between contemporaries or between an older man and a younger boy, usually an adolescent, was a phase which many Greek young men went through, that it was not a constant or one-way orientation, that sodomy is not always represented as being a part of it. In Macedonia, we know of homoerotic relationships between young boys, especially those in the group of Royal Pages. A malicious Greek visitor to Philip's court complained that his Companion-nobles were much too keen on male sex with each other, even though they were adults 'with beards': his description was plainly malicious, but it was surely an exaggeration, not a total invention. We should think of Alexander's sexuality, but not (in the prevailing modern sense) of his homosexuality: he had a Persian mistress, several occasional women and eventually, the three wives (two of these women, perhaps three, had children by him). Ancient sources (Plutarch, the Roman Curtius) describe the Persian eunuch Bagoas as one of his sexual partners. "Did oriental eunuchs do it in a different position?", Oliver asked, "I've been told they did." "There is no evidence."

"OK: for me, this sex-question is not the big one. Alexander had sexuality, he might love a male, he might love a woman. And he wasn't so unusual at the time." "No", I said, "although we don't happen to know of named male lovers for his other officers or for his early successors." "Do you know Johnny Depp?" Oliver interrupted, "He's a good friend, a good actor: he jokes with me that he won't be in this film because it will be nothing but sex. Why do people think that about this film without seeing it?" "Because of their image of a gay California and Hollywood; besides, there are vocal minorities in Greece who have a problem with the sex question, although it is so often a problem about themselves." In the film, Oliver's Alexander would have a sex life, but certainly not a one-way 'gay' or 'camp' one: the issue is admirably treated. To amuse him, I revealed how a Gay Book Club had once wrongly advertised my book as the "dashing story of the spellbinding young gay who conquered the world" and had sold thousands of it in a double offer with another book called "A Dutchman Unbuttons his Trousers." "I've got a Dutchman joining us as the Production Designer," Oliver replied with a smile, "would that be a way of marketing the film? We could run him as a B movie: do you still have B movies in your local cinemas?" He paused. "Plutarch says that Alexander said that sex and sleep made him realise he was mortal: is that correct?" I explained that we do not know that Alexander said such a thing, and a later source might have invented it. "OK, we'll leave all that out". It was Julius Caesar, not Alexander, who slept around with fellow-Romans' wives and the two men's sexualities were very different. Alexander was remembered as strongly opposed to rape, including the rape of female captives.

"Sex isn't the big issue: let's get back to Alexander's parents. What do we know of Olympias?" I tried, but I explained that much of it may be a stereotype or male slander: however, she surely did worship the god Dionysus. There even happens to be archaeological evidence now for Dionysiac worship by women up at Pella in Macedonia. "What did the women worshippers do?" "On one view, which I do not share, they did not even drink. In my view they drank, they danced, probably letting their hair down..." "Did they tear up animals?" "No, only in the tragedies and myths: Euripides' play, The Bacchae, was almost certainly written in Macedonia." "Then, they did not play with severed heads?" "No". He seemed thoughtful.

"Whom should I get to play all these people?" Oliver asked, quizzically, "We have been talking to Heath Ledger, but he has now dropped out on us: have you seen him? He's just been in The Four Feathers. Maybe he thinks Alexander is too imperialist. Who is right for it?" "Don't ask me: I haven't a clue: my film heroes stop with Alec Guinness". "Great actor, Guinness," Oliver mused, "we could have cast him as Aristotle: those old English Ealing comedies, they were great films too. When you have that mad look in your eye, Robin, you remind me of Peter Sellers. Nobody has ever been a comic actor like Sellers but we can't cast him in this one: imagine him as a Persian, with an accent." And, finally, we talked about Alexander's wives (we know so little about them), his debts to his tutor Aristotle (were they really so small?), his opinion of barbarians. Finally we talked of Philip, Alexander's father. "What do we know of their relationship?" So I retold the sources for Philip's disastrous last marriage to Eurydice, for the quarrels with Alexander and for his murder. "Do you agree with Professor Badian at Harvard that Alexander planned or willed it?" "No, but what do you think?" I answered, expecting the worst, as Oliver has given conspiracy-theories such a prominence in other films and Badian is Alexander's most famous modern historical critic. "Nor do I, but it's interesting if Alexander didn't realise, until much later, that there was a background to the murder, that the murderer Pausanias was said to be so aggrieved with Philip. What about Alexander's relations, though, with his father: were they difficult for him?" "There are enough hints in the sources for you to develop that line", I replied, "perhaps Alexander resented Philip and then stressed Zeus as his father. "So", Oliver answered, "if I go into Alexander's relations with Olympias and Philip, there is a gap there in the building which our imaginations need to fill?" "Certainly": I did not know that Moritz was urging the same line.

There had been no slackening in the pace, except when Oliver muddled the bits of paper and had to hunt for yet another question. He stopped, at last: "Do you want lunch?" It was nearly 5pm, after six hours grilling. Rob was called: there was a brief discussion about whether this lady or that lady had gone and about theatre tickets for the evening. "If we go downstairs now, we'll be private: nobody will notice us". Were we really so famous?

Olympias (Angelina Jolie) speaks out to her son Alexander (Colin Farrell) in a highly emotional scene.

Director Oliver Stone instructs King Philip (Val Kilmer) before his death in Aigai's theatre.

Olympias (Angelina Jolie), wearing her snake bracelet, embraces her boy Alexander (Connor Paolo).

Over our lunch-cum-supper, we talked more personally, of our schooling, our memory of our parents (like Philip and Olympias, Oliver's parents had quarrelled when he was young). I had the impression, soon to be refuted, of someone who had not had a big chance for several years. Like Gregory Peck, was he dreaming? When the wine came, could he pour it steadily? But it was I who was the more exhausted, after six hours of continuous questioning, in which nothing said earlier was forgotten by this sparring-partner who had certainly done his training. How *did* Macedonians swear at each other?

We returned upstairs, and Oliver suddenly asked me "what do you want out of all this?" I suppose I should have said squillions of dollars, an option taken out on my book which he was holding in his hand and some sort of right to withhold my name if the script and the film were awful. But on the way to meet him, I had decided on two more important conditions: "I want to ride in the front ten of every major cavalry charge involving Alexander and the Macedonians. And when my name is in the credits, I want it to be preceded with the words "and introducing...". Even Oliver was taken by surprise. "Do you even ride?" In fact, I have ridden since the age of 10 and horses are a non-negotiable part of my life. "That's no problem." I assured him, "it won't be half as hard as a day's foxhunting, and I've done that every winter for nearly fifty years." "But you can't expect "and introducing": there are rules about that, Robin, and you're not an actor. As for the cavalry, there'll be problems with insurance and safety: what happens if you fall off?" "I won't, and my family will sympathise with you, not sue you." "OK: I'll do it, if I possibly can. We'll have a Companion cavalryman from Oxford, a 'rebel on horseback'". Only after the event did I understand what these pregnant words meant. In his first film, Salvador, Oliver had filmed the left-wing guerrillas riding heroically on horseback against the Americans' tanks. Critics had complained at this over-affectionate image, 'rebels on horseback' galloping to their death. "You're mad, you know, but you've helped to give it life for me. You're a mixture of Ian Fleming and Peter Sellers. But we'll have to work on those long arms..."

So I left for Oxford, exhausted, as every other casting would eventually leave Oliver's intense presence. "Be sure you understand", he had insisted, "we are not making a history book. This is not a documentary. It is a dramatisation, though it should take history as its starting point. There will have to be compromises, because of time, money, drama, and space. If you can accept that, I'll try to keep explaining when we have to depart from that 'framework'. I'll have to run events together, and condense them, but I want to capture the spirit of it. Alexander killed off his historian Callisthenes: if you stay with it, I hope you won't kill me". In the encounters of the past thirty years, I had met with unpredictable questions: how did Greeks eat? how did they lie in bed? Alexander's sex-life was a hardy perennial, and everyone picked on Olympias. But I had never met the admission that Alexander was greater than a film-maker's ego, the frank discussion of the boundary between history and film-epic and the familiarity with the views of Badian, Tarn and Plutarch. Did he really have the grip to make it? How little I knew, and perhaps Oliver himself still did not know it, either. Anthony Hopkins, our actor as Ptolemy, had thought when first going to meet Oliver, he "would be going to meet a caveman." I had a very dif-

31

ferent impression: a man with a wide-angled lens, swinging from shot to shot, with a microscopic focus on detail, and a memory like an elephant. Technologically, it is I who live in the stone age, but I had not met a caveman at all: I had actually appreciated him. "By Ian Fleming, out of Peter Sellers…": what cavalryman could boast of such a pedigree?

A week later, I received a black and white postcard in Oxford: it showed the Cuban cavalry-riding in a charge with their flag fluttering in the centre. "Dear Robin," the handwritten message began on the back, "that could be you there, somewhere in the middle…". Historians are not easy to manipulate, but there are thank-you cards which are irresistible if the historian is a lover of horses.

Alexander (Colin Farrell) surveys his troops in battle order at Gaugamela.

4. SORTING OUT THE SCRIPT

Oliver went back to California, stopping in Cuba for a film-interview with Fidel Castro, himself an admirer of Alexander's generalship. On his return we fell into a working routine. His assistant, Rob, would ring and suggest a mutually convenient time and as Oxford is hours ahead of Los Angeles, it would be late in the evening after my University duties. To keep awake, I would watch some obscure movie on British television: Oliver would ring back, there would be a pause while he hunted for his handwritten notes and sometimes he would ask what I was watching. He usually knew the film and could fill me in with what would happen after I had switched off. Sometimes I had a critique of it too: "watch Paul Newman… the camerawork is not good when you see him walking to the bus… then the knife scene is excellent": it was for me to recall the ancient sources about Alexander, but he was a walking database on films.

The calls took at least an hour and ranged all over the subject. Sometimes, they concerned disputed events on Alexander's march: why did the Royal Pages plot against him? Why did he wait so long at Tyre in 331 BC before marching inland and fighting at Gaugamela? Like a film camera, the questions would then zoom in to objects and details, many of which I had to go off and track down. What did the Babylonian god Marduk look like? What were windows like in fourth century Greece (they were usually closed in with panels of wood)? How did ancient Greeks wipe their noses (probably, they rubbed them on the sleeves of their tunics)? Quite often, Oliver brought out the gaps in my own hazy notions of 'daily life'. "So Alexander had a male friendship with Hephaestion, a Persian mistress (Barsine) and an Iranian wife (Roxane), the Persian eunuch, and then two more Persian wives: who slept where?" I had never tried to imagine it: "would Roxane be in the same tent, or in another? Where did Hephaestion sleep? What about the final two wives?" There is a wider point of interest here. As historians, our responsibility is to study the surviving evidence: it guides what we write. For film-makers, precise questions force themselves forwards, irrespective of the evidence, when they try to visualise a scene. "How did Alexander keep Homer's epic poem, The Iliad, under his pillow? It's a very long poem: would it be written on one big scroll or on several? If there were several, were they all under his pillow or only one? If only one, where were the rest?" Repeatedly, I could imagine Oliver in another life as a most persistent lawyer. The question about the scrolls kept coming back at me.

Other questions probed modern historians' views of Alexander. "Is Peter Green's book about Alexander essentially Ernst Badian's view with a few more racy details and inter-connections?" Oliver had it just about right. "What is driving Brian Bosworth to call the Alexandrias, Alexander's city-foundations, "a new wave of barbarism from the West"? Why does he always have it in for Alexander, behind the smokescreen of 'objective' scholarship and 'realism'? Why does he still think that Alexander was trying to impose worship of himself as a god when he tried to introduce proskynesis? You've all refuted that already". In the 1980's, Maxwell O'Brien, a doctor, wrote a book ascribing acute alcoholism to Alexander, calling it the 'invisible enemy' which killed him. Certainly, Alexander drank heavily on occasions, sometimes throughout the night, but our word 'alcoholism' is not the right explanation. If an alcoholic means someone who drinks compulsively even when alone, who 'must' have a drink at all hours, Alexander was not an 'alcoholic', nor do Greeks seem to represent drinking as occurring in this addictive way or out of a social setting. Oliver had talked with O'Brien, as I had once in Oxford, where he came to lunch with a professor of Greek history who was himself quite open to the 'invisible enemy'. 'Temperance' was very much O'Brien's way in to the subject, but I did leave him and the professor returning to the martini bottle and swapping opinions on the way in which the Old Testament describes the physical and mental effects of drink. "We'll leave the Temperance Movement out of it", Oliver concluded. There is also the problem that some of the sources for Alexander's persistent drinking are unreliable, though doctors, trusting text books, take them too uncritically.

Religion and morals were major areas of discussion. "Which gods were in the 'Twelve Gods'?" - it is wrong to be too precise - "and would Dionysus be one of the gods whom Alexander honoured at his great altars when the army turned back in India?" In fact, Alexander is said to have cited the "anger of Dionysus" as the main reason for his murder of Cleitus and for his failure to go further into India. Historians have under-emphasised the importance of this belief for Alexander himself. "Was Dionysus the god of wine and excess?" We discussed how he was also a god of energy, release and life-giving forces: Oliver liked this perspective and it soon resurfaced in a script.

The Greeks' views of an after-life came up too (many Greeks did not believe in one). But some contemporaries implied that Alexander had not died: he had 'departed from among men': he was a god and, some people later imagined, he had become a star - a real star in the heavens, not a star on the screen. What about Persian religion and what about their prophet Zoroaster? For a while, in the later scripts, Aristotle would talk to the young boys, I thought rather well, about the opposing gods of Good and Evil in Persian religion. The Titans also attracted attention, as they soon did in the scenes of Philip's visit to the ancient cave-paintings below the Pella palace. What were their names? Then, the questions would broaden, as if Oliver himself was curious to know answers. What were the main differences between ancient Greek values and Christian values? Humility, respect for the 'poor' as spiritually meritorious – if these questions are to be answered in five minutes flat, they keep you on your toes. "OK, but was Apollo homosexual?" I forgot that Apollo did have a passion for the boy called Hyacinthus: Oliver remembered. Above all, we kept coming back to Aristotle. What was this supreme Being of his, the 'Unmoved Mover'?

These questions, and dozens of others, took us on through a night-time quiz-game, played twice a week or more until late summer. On most nights, there was a word or two about the need to hurry. Dino and the rivals were still putting out their press-releases and were now threatening to start their filming first. More and more there was talk about Colin Farrell. No, I had never seen him; no, we do not really know what Alexander looked like. Arguably, he was not too tall, and apparently he was shorter than Hephaestion. The images on his Successors' coins give us some idea, but they are idealised. I stressed, as usual, the importance of the 'Alexander Mosaic' which is now in the Naples Museum and is a copy of a lost masterpiece by one of Alexander's court artists. It is stylised too, but it defines Alexander's features for many modern viewers: brown-eyed, angular and brown haired with lighter dashes in the mosaic. "Highlighting?" Oliver wondered.

I had no idea that as a result an 'Oliver Stone: script draft 1' existed in July 2002. Reading it with hindsight, I see how so much we had debated had become interwoven. There were scenes with Callisthenes, Alexander's personal historian; the battles in Outer Asia against the Scythians became a major affair; Roxane appeared, as we had discussed, on horseback, "her long black hair flashing free of headwear"; in a very neat scene of Oliver's, Ptolemy stops to reflect on his purchase of volumes of Olympias' "authentic letters" for his library (all the letters we now have are later fakes). In India, the wounding of Bucephalas in battle is correctly separated from the later wounding of Alexander at his siege of the Indian town Multan. This disaster, and his recovery, became prolonged scenes in his relations with his soldiers. Near the end, in Babylon, we flashed back to the oracle of Zeus in the oasis of Siwah, a cardinal moment in Alexander's self-awareness and his sense of his divine parentage. Only at the end, after Alexander dies, do we have the scene which is now the film's opening: "To whom? To whom do you leave the kingdom?"

In reply, co-producer Thomas Schühly was ecstatic by letter from Germany: "brilliantly conceived and written... Homeric... showing peaks which underline impressively your outstanding and ingenious narrative talent". Of course Thomas had more suggestions. In Babylon, where we meet a priest, "could we not introduce Jahweh too, the god of the Jews" (indeed there were Jews in Babylon) "and Jews who would refuse to bow down to Alexander... we could add a couple of Nietzsche-lines?" "Instead of the Persepolis scene... why not show some great and thrilling hunting scene? Burning down a temple... how does this show the darker sides of Alexander's soul? ...I think Alexander's "darker nature" lies in his archaic and tigerish lust for hunting down dangerous animals and even more dangerous men on the battlefield... The Dionysian side of his character was not sex... it was blood, killing and death... Parmenion makes a very intriguing question... "Is it the lust for war which drives Alexander to the East?" I admit I hadn't seen this point yet...".

Stone Draft 1 was very exciting, clearly, but not only Schühly saw the problems. It was a third longer than the final script and the locations had multiplied, adding an Indian siege, Persepolis and Siwah. The final Act Three tailed away in haste; the scene at Siwah (where Alexander asked, 'who killed my father?') was "more Hamlet than history". There was also, still, a scene of a female Dionysiac orgy in a ravine in Macedonia. Schühly loved it, as he loved the newly-devised scene with Philip and the mythical frescoes in the cave below Pella, "the movies of the ancient world". But, he suggested, "Alexander was not only shocked" when he saw his mother at a Dionysiac ritual holding the limbs of a severed slave: for Thomas, "he was also shocked by a certain excitement". Historians, Greek audiences and many others, I insisted, would have been shocked by the scene's very existence. In real life, Greek maenads are never known to have torn humans or animals to pieces: it is all a mythical story, and Mary Renault's novels had wrongly set it in Olympias's Macedonia and misled Oliver.

Between Schühly's philosophy and my facts in Oxford, Oliver was no doubt feeling bombarded. In the year 2000, when writing on his work's relation to history, Oliver had stated: "Especially now, having been through so many accusations about my integrity these past thirteen-some years, I'm perhaps over-careful, too much so to strike with the necessary lightning fist of the dramatist, now spent in "the slough of information". Was Stone Draft 1 losing the lightning in a 'slough' of Lane Fox detail? In August, Oliver disappeared to Thailand and the phone calls became shorter: he was excited at the locations for filming which Thailand offered. A 'Stone Draft 2' came and went without me and in October it was followed by 'Stone Draft 3'. Very few people saw it, although Moritz Borman liked its new, raw power, which could hold an audience. I know it only from Schühly's impassioned reactions: it seems that it could have been captioned, "The lightning fist strikes back".

"Draft 3 reminds me of Fellini's Satyricon", Thomas wrote back in haste, "with its steamy and hot atmosphere of decadent and decaying times… a final big feast of Dionysus's destructive forces". Relations between Alexander and Olympias had evidently become overheated; acutely, Schühly pointed to the excessive proportion of 'indoor' scenes, to the Roman atmosphere ("call it Caligula, not Alexander", and then it would be "just brilliant"), and to the 'passivity' of Alexander's 'psychologizing' which could not possibly explain the action, or a fraction of it, which had made the historical Alexander so great. Plainly, Oliver was still pushing the boundaries, casting round for what might work and what did not. "I am amazed at the uproar my films have caused since 1986", Oliver had written only recently, "but only a moron would consider them documentaries… But neither are they to be excused as 'only a film' from 'only an entertainer'. I write and direct with the purpose of seeking out the truth as best I can, using the tools of the dramatist… I have no overriding ideology beyond that of, let's say, 'common sense'… I would not know how to motivate a convincing drama from ideology." A historical adviser can only advise: dramatists are dramatists.

By November, Dionysus was being tamed once again by common sense and rational Apollo. A month later, the telephone-calls were back in force, and I felt a new urgency. What had changed, of course, was the film's chances of being filmed, thanks to Moritz Borman's continuing leap of faith and the beginnings of the financing by distributors, starting with Pathé films in France. There was a renewed attention to fact. "Let's go back to Dionysus: what did Macedonian maenads actually do?" As Draft 3 became Draft 4, the maenads faded more peacefully into the background. As a spectacle, the scene in the ravine might have worked, but as history, not myth, it was completely unsupported, and

King Philip (Val Kilmer) shows the cave-paintings below Pella's palace to his young son Alexander (Connor Paolo).

The labours of Herakles drawn on the cave walls below Pella's palace.

Aristotle (Christopher Plummer), Alexander's tutor and the most intelligent of all the Greeks.

Oliver's common sense now threw it out. Roxane, instead, stayed centre-stage. "Did she really poison one of Alexander's other Persian wives?", Oliver wondered. I had forgotten this allegation, though Oliver had found it at the end of Plutarch's life: it may be a rumour, put about by her many enemies. "Might she have poisoned Hephaestion?" Nobody says so, but the idea had a certain poetic justice, so it surfaced, aired as a possibility by Ptolemy, in the final script. "When Alexander first sees her," Oliver asked, "what is she like?" I had this vision of Roxane, dressed in furs and hunting-robes, galloping out from a castle, shooting arrows at wild animals as she passed. The riding, at least, had been in Script Draft One, and Rosario, yet to be cast, would have risen to the challenge. But Oliver saw through it: "do we know she was pro-hunting, or is this only propaganda for blood sports?"

The gods were also being tightened up. Repeatedly we had discussed the visit to the oracle of Zeus in the Siwah oasis on Egypt's border. As a result of it Alexander had liked it to be known that he was the 'begotten son of Zeus'. This theme developed from the words with which the oracle's priest greeted him: were they prearranged words or a spontaneous greeting to his new ruler, the Pharaoh of Egypt? Oliver had his doubts: "it is all going to be muddled up with Christ as son of God, and the audience won't believe it. Let's keep it on the margins, and use Ptolemy to cast some doubt on it". Alexander's visit to Troy and the visit to Siwah were vital for Alexander's self-image, but they would have to be raised only in dialogue and by Ptolemy in the voice over.

During the autumn, I had thought a bit more about the Titans. "How would Macedonians have talked about the passions", Oliver asked, "and the ferocity in a man? Nowadays we'd say it was 'in' someone - in his genes perhaps: did Greeks have an idea of inborn savagery?" It was then that I remembered the finding of a famous papyrus in one of the tombs at Derveni on Macedonia's borders. In the 1960's, fragments were found here of an anonymous text, the only papyrus-find ever in Greece, which gave a most unusual sort of theology. In its version, the Titans try to kill the baby Dionysus: Zeus scorches them with a thunderbolt and then mixes their ashes into the ancestors of the human race. The Titans are not imprisoned: these old and violent creatures are still in each one of us. Oliver liked the idea; it could unify the film's scenes of myth, its scenes of Alexander's ferocity and Ptolemy's final memories of him. For me, there was the satisfaction of taking the most obscure text of Greek theology, found in Macedonia, and putting it into a big film. I started to work it in everywhere: "give the audience a break," Oliver retorted, "or do you want this film to be called The Dust of the Titans?"

Aristotle, too, needed shaking up. "What did Aristotle think about the myths?", Oliver asked me. Again, the question is not easy but after talking with my Oxford colleague in ancient philosophy, Paolo Crivelli, I went back to passages in Aristotle's works. They show that he believed that once upon a time the world had been through a great flood during winter and that a previous age of civilisation had all been washed away. The only survivors of it were shepherds and simple people in the mountains who had escaped the rising waters. Their descendants were the sole guardians of the lost 'ancient wisdom', but being simple people they had distorted it into myths. Global catastrophe, a lost wisdom: it sounded just what an American audience would love, so I hurried to alert Oliver. Better still, Aristotle thought that such a winter flood would happen again and would wash us all out. In a wet English winter, since global warming, it was easy to believe him. Oliver was much more sceptical. "You're telling me that Aristotle thought that the people up in the hills have hung onto an ancient wisdom which the rest of us have lost? Hell, in the hills round here, they're against blacks, against Jews and against gays. Aristotle should have interviewed them". "But Oliver, aren't you worried when Aristotle says that the world is sure to be washed out all over again?" "Robin, in everything else you tell me about this guy, he's got it wrong, so if he says we're going to be flooded, I feel much more confident: he'll have got that wrong too." Plainly, like the floods, Oliver's spirits were rising.

With Aristotle put in his place, it was clearly time for a Stone Draft 4 to come down for scrutiny in Oxford. In April we met up in Pinewood and the Oliver I found was significantly different from the Oliver of a year before. He was just back from a reconnaissance trip in Pakistan and India, Ladakh and the Himalayas with his newly recruited producer Iain Smith. Shots from this trip's scenery would be used in the backgrounds of Alexander's march into Scythia and Central Asia. The thin moustache was gone, so was a kilo or two of weight and there was a new urgency (and a new grey hat) about his person. On the way down 'Broccoli Road' to the vast '007 Studio' which would soon become Babylon, he was already impatient that I was walking too slowly. All around us trucks were dumping the debris of the last James Bond set, with the detached indifference of a funeral parlour. The Bond films, in my view, are awful, but eight months later, the same dumping would begin for the wonders of Babylon, Pella and the Alexandria Library. In exchange for a £1 coin, I signed a promise of confidentiality: Script Draft 4 (the first I had seen) would follow, within a week.

Outsiders have often described the shock of first reading a film-script on a subject of which they are already knowledgeable. Its connecting paragraphs give details of sets and objects ("a DOZEN CONCUBINES from the Palace harem nervously await the new CONQUEROR, bursting through he doors, sculpted with huge fish mouths and RUTTING DEER…"): motives and body language are spelled out ("ROXANE, dressed for her virgin experience, stands in the outer doorway, shocked to see HEPHAESTION in tears. When she sees the new RING on Alexander's finger, her eyes show a ferocious jealousy, a quality which Alexander despises most of all, fear"). Above all, historical people are given words which they never said, spaced out at wide intervals as actors' parts on a page. Not knowing the conventions, I could not suspend the historian's basic question: "where is the evidence?" It all looked phoney.

On a second or third reading, as others have experienced, the conventions become clearer and the drama can begin to be read on its own fictional terms. I still did not understand how important the connecting paragraphs are: "The sounds of the wedding below are heard in a gloomy CHAMBER filled with artefacts of bone, skull and fur…" Here, concisely, are instructions for sound-effects ("faint sounds"), for set design ("below"… "gloomy") and for set-dressing ("bone, skull and fur"). "ROXANE, back to us, she is now naked to him, her skin the colour of amber:" that sounded promising, but the female casting would be glad to know it in advance. "Alexander wears an expression like a mythic hero, always in conflict. At war are twin views of himself…" Here are specific orders for an actor on how to play the scene: confronted with a stark naked starlet, could he really be a divided soul? Historians are used to a time-line that moves straight and keeps events in the right order. To my eye, Oliver's script jumped around, whereas the parts, of course, were arranged in an all-important dramatic inter-relation. Some of it did slowly become clearer to me on the page. There was a relation between Ptolemy's narration and the scenes to which we flash, and also between the switching from Alexander's wedding with Roxane to Philip's earlier, disastrous plan to replace Alexander's mother Olympias and marry Eurydice ("Pregnant already, the little whore..", says Olympias). But I still took each section separately, unable to read it 'filmically' or to see what Oliver would later explain to me as a web not of flashbacks but of 'parallel stories'. The web reinforces, and deepens, the emotions and reactions in the script-directions, and the 'parallel stories' are not just flashbacks. They are a running psychological commentary.

Even when read in my pedantic way, the actors' text had strengths. There was a real force in the scenes and quarrels in Macedonia: Ptolemy's narrative was a key, though it needed tidying and correcting: it was neat that we were warned to be wary of his version right at the start ("this is the great consolation of biography - it allows us to lie") and it was dramatic, at the end, when he dropped his guard and said what he really thought ("I never believed in his dream! None of us ever did"). The presentation of Alexander surprised me: I had expected, from Oliver, something uniformly dark and excessively conspiratorial who would surely be poisoned at the end. With amusement, I could imagine minimalist historians jumping too quickly to conclusions and writing off the film as one-sided hero-worship because they would take all Ptolemy's views as Oliver's own. There was no one-sided 'conspiracy theory'. There was greatness, there was psychological drama, there was a terrifying ferocity. The sex was excellently handled, it was certainly not 'Caligula in Babylon'. The directions for the battle scenes seemed made for me: "All that horsepower, ready to charge, is hard to contain… precise signals are passed to the COMMANDERS at the head of each WEDGE OF 200 CAVALRY… the HORSEMEN take their mounts inward in unison. It becomes a race!"

On the other hand, there were still plenty of false notes. The names of the minor characters were either impossible or wrong for their place of origin: Greek personal names are often very specific to a region. Ptolemy's dates and geography slipped around too often, even if he was now aged nearly 80. Details of diplomacy and power structures had, inevitably, lost touch with history: Oliver was not a specialist in this period. Too often, a title or a phrase was Roman rather than Greek, an interesting reminder that the Roman world is so much more familiar in American films than the Greek one. The action dialogue was less problematic, with only the odd false note about gods or oaths. But reflective soliloquies or abstract conversations are so much harder. Again, it was interesting how Oliver's attempt to give a sense of Alexander as someone apart, with a different view of the future, would sometimes result in phrases with a Christian or biblical overtone ("fear not…").

Oliver rang, and was wary: "are you appalled by it?" After so many years, and such detail, he had every right to be proprietorial: "No", I said, "I give it a 'B'", like professors in his American University past. "How far down do the letters go?" he simply asked. "D would be awful," I replied, "E worse, and F means 'Fail'". Four months later, on the Moroccan desert-set, he would ask me if the first shots were now B plus: his heads of department would sometimes be given an 'F'. Most directors, I now realise, would have simply ended the bother of ringing me. Not so Oliver. "OK," he replied, "how do I get an 'A'?" So we went through some of the weaker pages, and soon we came to a speech for Alexander as he is looking out from the balcony at Babylon. It is a key moment, a first hint of what the conqueror might think of the future, and it sounded wrong: "A new wind is blowing across the face of the world... they want change, Hephaestion." "In 1987", I told him, "I saw a film called 'Wall Street' in which a character called Gordon Gekko made a stirring speech on a factory floor about 'change' and 'freedom' to the workers in a company which he was about to sell off. Alexander sounds like Gordon Gekko in Babylon: it will have to change". There was a pained silence. "Robin, do you know who wrote that film?" "I haven't the slightest idea." "I did."

In a way, it made my argument stronger, and six weeks later Oliver asked me to meet again in London. It was to be the same hotel, the same table, the same dining room, but this time, we went through the main 'problem pages'. There was even the same sort of notebook, and of course the same sort of tussle. Sometimes a character had lived on too long: in the film, Alexander's general Parmenion survives for three extra years, and the attested conspiracies against Alexander become merged together. "But they are not narrated in sequence in Arrian, either," the main ancient narrative, Oliver countered. True enough, but the displacement there is not so marked. "OK, but if they go back in, something else goes out." We discussed authentic names ("but don't forget, it was I who invented the name Gordon Gekko and you remember it"): we pinpointed problems with Aristotle, who sounded untrue to the philosopher's own ideas. And we returned to 'Alexander on Wall Street'. "OK, suggest a different tack." "You have Hephaestion looking anxiously at Alexander, worrying that he's going too far. Think of him as beginning to be hard to be with, of becoming impossible, of standing too high. When have you seen people like that?" "At the Oscars, maybe: or after a great performance, like Tom Cruise in 'Born on the Fourth of July'. Do you know who wrote that one, Robin?" "OK, then, think 'Alexander wins an Oscar in 1985'; think 'Alexander as Tom Cruise'. "We nearly cast him for the part, back in 1997".

"Can you send me some script for all this?", he suddenly asked. My job had simply been to comment and be consulted: directors do not exactly look for historians to write script for them. "I'm open to any suggestions: you send them, I'll harvest anything we can use". My brief was now to concentrate on Ptolemy whose narration could be changed more easily, on Aristotle, and on Alexander's forward-looking speeches. The script was certainly not yet set in Stone. By now, had I realised, the sets were almost chosen, the locations under way; Colin had a script and so did all the others who were coming on board. Most directors would have left the script as it was, but among the multiplying pressures, Oliver kept at it until 'Draft 4' was nearly 'Draft 5'. With my pupil Tamsin Cox at her laptop, I

Alexander (Colin Farrell) in his campaign tent, decorated with the historic star symbol of the Macedonian kingdom.

The Macedonian army marches in triumph through Babylon.

Cassander (Jonathan Rhys Meyers), so often at odds with Alexander.

sent page after page of comment and text down the system to the imperturbable Rob. The Babylon speech changed and Ptolemy stayed historically on target. Aristotle conformed more closely to his written works, taking his final shape after discussions across the lunch table with my Oxford colleagues. In the end, new script was wired to the willing Christopher Plummer, Aristotle's actor, barely two days before being filmed. While I was on set, small corrections of fact were dictated by me to Rob Wilson: then, during the filming, the proposed text of each forthcoming scene was couriered to me in Oxford for reactions and comments in case of an obvious blind spot. The exchanges continued throughout the filming. While teaching my pupils the evidence about Ptolemy or Olympias, I was sending fictional words to Oliver for their namesakes to perform.

If I stress this process, it is not in order to overestimate my role. "The foetus is the script", Oliver had said elsewhere, "but it comes out and grows. The baby changes shape. It's very much your own, but the look is a little bit different than you originally imagined." The structure is Oliver's, the 'web' of the plot and most of the dialogue are his. But the long gestation of a script has seldom been recorded, and I was the paediatrician. So many 'historical advisers' have run into the opposite problem. Recently, the distinguished historian Anthony Beevor found himself 'consulted' on Jean Jacques Annaud's film 'Enemy at the Gates', but Beevor's history-book on Stalingrad had exposed the story around which the entire film's climax was constructed: it was false Russian propaganda. Nobody showed him a script in advance and on set, he was expected simply to approve the film's 'historicity' as "based on a true story". When such directors refer to historians as 'nuisances' or as 'dry' in contrast to their own 'creativity', it is they who (rightly) become ridiculous because they, and their distributors, also crave the stamp of 'historical accuracy' or 'based on historical truth'. For 'Gladiator', my classical colleague Kathy Coleman sent pages of expert comments on the script, pointing out the historical errors and the falsity in all the scenes of gladiatorial combat and Roman history. No attention was paid to her: she never had any access to the set: she wanted her name off the credits, but (typically) the film wanted to cite her by name. Such Hollywood films want it both ways: "based on a true story" with a respected historian credited, but actually formed by self-willed directors and ignorant, historically untrained script-writers. Kathy's advice, circulated to classicists by the internet, was that the hope of giving historical guidance to a Hollywood film is a fantasy. So much has been said and written about Oliver Stone's 'disrespect' for history that it is worth stressing here that within his chosen dramatic limits, his attention to historical advice about 'Alexander' was constant, and serious. Events are sometimes merged or re-ordered, but these changes were not done in ignorance or out of disrespect. The eight or more drafts often contained a scene, correctly placed, which had to be cut or shifted in a later version. Throughout, Oliver was insistent that it is the script which makes or breaks a film. So many directors of epics forget this crucial truth: 'Alexander' is a very strong drama, with a real epic range, but one of its strengths is its strong relation to the historical record.

In real life, Alexander's 'historical adviser', Callisthenes, became increasingly disenchanted with Alexander's drinking and his favour for 'barbarian' customs. He is said,

45

perhaps truly, to have conspired against his 'director' and he was put to death by Alexander for the attempt. I had no cause to conspire against Oliver and the result is a script with a much greater reference to history. If he was going to kill me, it would be solely at my own discretion, by my charging on horseback too close to one of his elephants.

Hephaestion (Jared Leto), Alexander's closest friend in the world.

5. PLAYING ALEXANDER

The script had a slow, hard birth, but everybody knew that the film would be still-born without the right star as Alexander. The actor would have to be young, preferably in his 20's: not too tall, but sufficiently strong and agile for a huge action role of battles, riding horses bareback and killing: he would have to span the years from Alexander's adolescence to his deathbed, and be scarred by experience; he would have to lead and inspire an army and stand out among his co-starring officers; he would be on centre-screen for most of the film and he would have to react to four or five different cultures on his way East; there would be sex, suffering and murder, the murder of one of his senior generals. He would also have to do justice to the theme which ran through Oliver's drama: the relations between Alexander's parents which remain the 'parallel story' in his career, especially the influence of his mother. What, too, should he look like? Bits of text from antiquity which describe Alexander's looks are stylized or symbolic and are fullest in the legendary 'Alexander Romance' which developed unhistorically long after his death. Some of them compare Alexander to a 'lion', and hence they say his hair was 'tawny', but even if it was, how fair is 'tawny'? The best sources are coins, mosaics and paintings, but almost every coin portrait of Alexander was struck after his death The mosaics are copies of lost original paintings whose details and colours may have been changed. The one contemporary painting which may be of Alexander, on the Royal Tomb at Vergina, is disputed and even if it is him, it is damaged and only shows him when young. When alive, Alexander had a truly Hollywood concern for his own image. He appointed great artists to dominate each section of it, one for the sculptures, one for the paintings, one for the coins and gems. What we still see is shaped by their ideal filters.

There is an advantage for a director in this lack of evidence. Film goers and historians may have their personal image of Alexander, but they cannot be sure that they are right about his eye or hair colour. What, though, if the actor for Alexander is extremely well known? Can we then suspend disbelief? But if the film is to be a big hit, 'Alexander' cannot be cast with an unknown actor, able and fresh from a theatre. Could Tom Cruise have done it in the mid 1990's or was he already too established? In my view, Heath Ledger lacked the range: from spring 2002 he was not even an option. Luhrmann and di Laurentiis were publicising Leonardo di Caprio as their choice, but di Caprio was said to be waiting until he had read the script: it would surely have put him off, and anyway his looks were much too soft. Oliver kept searching far and wide, auditioning young hopefuls from Britain. But his trusted agent, Bryan Lourd, was insisting he should have a look at a young Irish star on the up, the twenty six year old Colin Farrell: Colin was cast in 'Dare Devil'.

Oliver duly asked Colin to join him for dinner at Michaels, the smart 'star' restaurant in Santa Monica. Colin was away in Mexico when the invitation reached him; he recalled for me how he turned up 'informally', which meant in a pair of diesel jeans after a drink or two to celebrate what had already, in his words, been a 'good day'. Even eighteen months later, he remembered the cocktails which he had Oliver order for him: first a Baldhead, then a Goldie. The dinner, he remembers, was 'loud': Oliver remembers rather more, glasses being dropped and broken and the other guests in the room looking round and wondering whom on earth Oliver Stone was with. Oliver left, thinking that here was yet another young Irishman, raw, untamed but was he Alexander in the making? Except for one thing: he could have matched Alexander's drinking, cup for cup, and he would certainly have been fit to fight Persia in the morning, especially if they had followed Greek practice and mixed water into the wine.

Dinner was followed by a breakfast down at Shutters Hotel, to which Moritz Borman was also invited. He had not quite expected Colin's 'Dare Devil' appearance: rough jeans, a closely shaven head. But Moritz was extremely positive, liking the guest's energy: "you've found your Alexander". For the moment, Oliver kept his options open, unwilling to close them without a comparison with other candidates put to him.

As other possible castings disappointed, Oliver decided to give the Irish boy a screen test in a warehouse location in Los Angeles. This time, Colin arrived with his sister. He comes from a very close Irish family of three brothers and sisters and his links with Dublin are still very strong. His elder brother teaches at a performing arts school there to which the tearaway Colin had been attached in his late teens, in the hope of fixing him to a career. Since his contact with Hollywood, his level-headed sister Claudine has been his full-time assistant and guiding light. To prepare him for the screen-test, she encouraged him to watch a tape of Richard Burton as Alexander. It is not a great performance, but it did help to give a little of the history and the period.

For Colin, an audition for a part was something from his past. For two years, directors had simply offered him his leading roles, so much so that "I felt like a thief". The sums paid to him seemed "ridiculous... they made no sense". But this time, the role was different, not just for "love on the screen: Alexander, Oliver Stone, they are chances you never expect to be offered. I had so much respect for Oliver, probably why I had overplayed it at the dinner". With Claudine's support he had decided to play the famous speech by Shakespeare's Mark Antony, "Friends, Romans and countrymen, lend me your ears". Make up was rudimentary ("eyeshadow with a sponge", Colin remembers), the set was only a wooden stage with a white backcloth and the audience was Oliver, Moritz Borman and Oliver's assistant, Rob Wilson. Colin was fitted with shiny black armour, a wig of blond curls and lace-up boots and began by declaiming his chosen lines. Oliver then gave him pages of his script in progress (Stone Draft One) and typically, warned him they were only a draft in progress... Colin read a range of lines, generous lines to his army and fiercer lines in which he tells his mutinous troops to go home. His costumes varied from one cloak to another and his voice rose classically at the end of each phrase. He had opted to read in 'Received Pronunciation', not Irish or American: "wherever did he learn to speak English?", Claudine found herself wondering in the audience. From the back of the room, Oliver would declaim supporting parts to help Colin on his way. "Four more rivers to cross," Oliver can be heard on cue on the tape, "and a million of the buggers ahead of us..." Colin picks up the scene, with a certain passion. "Pay them, and let them get out..." It was certainly not what he was thinking. For eight hours, he was taken through one change of mood after another: he had to look thoughtful, then dreamy, then inspiring, then impassioned and awesome. Oliver kept pushing him, seeing what he could draw out. On tape, the takes have a germ of the qualities which Oliver would appreciate, the combination of fierceness and emotion with an unexpected softness in the eyes. Colin was not Irish for nothing, and he also still had Alexander's youth.

Colin left, exhausted, but knowing that it had been one of the great days of his life. Claudine thought it 'amazing', and had seen "a new Colin" being teased out. His roles in Dare Devil still had to be finished off and there was plenty of work coming, so Colin tried to tell himself 'I don't care', and simply to enjoy "the promise of what I did not know might happen". He would be upset, but he would never forget this eight-hour marathon. Then, CAA Casting called him round to watch the results with Oliver, Bryan and Colin's agent Josh Lieberman. To Colin, the footage looked down-beat, "me in a bad wig", but Oliver took him by the shoulder, and suddenly, he knew he had the part. Oliver warned him of the scale of it and the physical hazards it would bring. Colin was not concerned. "Fear", he told him, "is rot". Oliver was so taken with the remark that he used it in his script, giving it to big Craterus (Rory McCann) as he steadies his men on first seeing war-elephants in India.

The script, the film-finance, the locations: all had to be sorted out and in fact nearly twelve more months would pass. Meanwhile Oliver saw his star becoming better and better known. 'Phone Booth', 'Dare Devil', 'The Recruit' built on the impact of 'Tigerland': would Colin allow his agents to renegotiate the original deal? Unusually, they did not, a show of loyalty which was crucial for the film's costing. In spring 2003, when the producers drew up tighter budgets, Colin's basic contract even had to be scaled down. Meanwhile, other studios were willing to offer him so much more for film parts which he knew "would not be worth the Kodak they were printed on." Colin was establishing a track-record of bringing big box-office profits, Hollywood's standard of value, but 'Alexander' was the challenge of a lifetime, which could lift or sink him to new levels. So for nearly a year, he held true to the offer. By April 2003, five months before filming, he began to stand back and prepare his mind. Alexander's era was so far away from anything he had ever done: Colin does have two words of ancient poetry tattooed on his arms, but they are in Latin ('Seize the day': 'Carpe Diem'), originating more than three hundred years after Alexander. He began to read Greek poetry in translation, Sophocles and the other tragedians (whose texts Alexander himself had once asked to be sent to him in Asia) and of course, the all-important Homer. Above all, he read carefully through Script Draft 4, twenty pages at a time. It took him three and a half hours, twenty cigarettes and four beers, and at once, he recognised the emotional intensity in it. "His failures," Ptolemy concludes, "were greater than other men's successes": might that be true of me too, Colin wondered, when I finish this part? It was a much more intelligent script than anything sent to him before. Alexander, he concluded, had "wished to make a reality out of what others could not even see as a possibility." Could he do it too?

Irish actors sometimes bring a warmth which many English actors lack, and American film-history owes so much to them, whether James Cagney or Alec Guinness, Brando, even, and John Huston. In July, Colin was over in his native Dublin for a script-rehearsal with Oliver and other members of the fast-growing cast. He then passed through London for a visit to the British Museum with his film-mother Olympias, Angelina Jolie ("on July 21, Colin was seen kissing her on the neck," the star-gazing magazines decided). Then, he withdrew back to California for several planned weeks in the countryside "to clear his thoughts." He bought a caravan: he settled north of L.A. in a valley of avocado trees, about five hectares big. Bananas grew over his caravan site, "like Jamaica", he remembers, and he slung a hammock among the trees and vines. Among the calls of the crickets and the hiss of the sprinkler system, he continued to study the script and to master his lines. He found that he was merging into the part "by osmosis... after drifting asleep, bits of the role became clearer to me... I always work this way, drifting off maybe for thirty seconds, even among friends, and returning with a clearer grasp of a line or two." He also embarked on his first military training, some of which, too, was to be learned with his eyes shut.

In his schooldays Colin had enjoyed football and basketball, but had hated gym. Now, he was pitched into combat-fighting with a female Body Coach, horse-riding with a Horse-master and military theory with an American ex-marine. The riding was the most difficult and the most fun. He had played one cowboy role, in the badly-received 'American Outlaws', and down in Austin, Texas, he had taken lessons for it on a 21-year old horse, with a trainer who had once taught John Wayne. But as 'Alexander' he was to ride one of the big black Dutch Friesian horses which the film's horsemaster, Ricardo Cruz Moral, had cleverly bought in Italy to play Alexander's beloved warhorse, Bucephalas. When they were bought, they were barely broken, and certainly not for the noise of a film crowd. First in California, then in Spain, Colin's riding skills had to be learned all over again. He would practice holding a spear on a quad bike, then on a horse; he would learn to trot bareback and even to make the big Friesian horses rear up on their hind legs. Naturally agile, he had an Irish talent for the job. If his film-career ever fails, he should train, in my view, as a jockey.

In the orchard, he had important visitors. Oliver would come up from the city to test his muscles and to take him, script in hand, through most of the lines. The film's Military Director, Dale Dye, will meet us later, but he too was up with Colin, seating him at a low table and beginning to tune him into battle-strategy and military leadership. By setting out twigs and bottle-caps on the table, Colin was to learn the basic tactics for the film's vast battle of Gaugamela. With their help he would learn to 'refuse his left wing', to strike inwards from the right and even to arrange the pieces with his eyes shut. The aim was to feel the flow of the action, so that he could lead his men with conviction and experience.

Colin Farrell in the lion helmet which is modelled on a sculpted ancient image of Alexander on horseback.

In the Persian Harem in Babylon, Alexander (Colin Farrell) first sees the eunuch Bagoas.

As the battle would be filmed in short, separate shots, the importance of this overview was perhaps more symbolic than real. But Colin took the main point: "a breakthrough on the right, whereas the enemy went for the loot". Could the motorbike star of Dare Devil really learn to stand out as a leader and a shining example? Dale Dye was making him learn a memory-trick to help him: "Jedd J Buklet, III." "What on earth was that?", I asked him in a bar in Thailand, four months later. "Each letter stands for a leadership quality," he replied, "Justice, Enthusiasm, Dependability, Decision, Judgement, Bearing, Understanding, Knowledge, Loyalty, Enthusiasm, Tact, Ingenuity, Inspiration and hell – I've forgotten the last 'I'." "Ireland?", I suggested, and with Alexander's approval, we drank to it.

'Jedd' could guide Colin, but he could not create an Alexander. The energy which came out in the first filmed scenes of battle was not unexpected, but the personal dominance was real 'star' quality. As in the screen test, Colin could change to a softness in his eyes for the early scenes with his mother and imply the suffering which even Alexander, Oliver believed, had experienced in his turbulent family. But nobody expected the emotional engagement, the flexibility and street-wise thoughtfulness which Colin now brought to the part. "I've wept litres," he told me, on the eve of the big elephant battle-scene in India, three months into the schedule, "seven-eighths of them off camera". In September and October, the filming in Morocco had mostly been scenes of battle and triumph: Colin wished he could replay the first ones when he had felt most under pressure. "Nobody can type-cast how to play a king... I began by declaiming too much and straining for the big gesture... I should have been more like one of the others...". But the scene of Philip's murder had gone well and he came back to England more confident.

At Pinewood in a wet English winter, the intensity began. The least of it was that Colin had to exchange kisses with a eunuch Bagoas (Francisco Bosch) and to be battered, then loved by the irrepressible Roxane (Rosario Dawson). He is admirably matter-of-fact about the film's few sexual moments: "like all the rest of us, Alexander had sexuality, and in the context of his society and Greek culture, he would express it, when young, with another young man. It was a phase. Keep our modern labels away from him: 'homosexual', 'heterosexual', 'bisexual'. And keep it in perspective: the sex is a very small part of this film. I'm not playing some sort of 'gay prince' in a sexual counter-culture: that's miles from Alexander". His matter-of-factness had even helped others. On screen for the first time in his life, the dancer Francisco Bosch (Bagoas) had to exchange a kiss on the lips with Colin. He started to freeze, until Colin pushed him towards him and told him "think of it like having a cigarette". What does he think of Plutarch's statement in the ancient life of Alexander, that "he used to say that only sex and sleep reminded him he was a mortal"? Colin countered me quickly: "did he really wish to be reminded? And do Plutarch, or his ancient sources, really report Alexander's own words? Anyway, I'd envy him both of his reminders..." No sooner had Olympias (Angelina Jolie) been cast than the popular press pointed out that she and Colin both shared the same astrology-sign (Gemini), both had a young child as a new responsibility (Angelina had adopted her little son Maddox) and both liked action and risk (Angelina had just played Lara Croft). At Pinewood, Colin found himself playing the son to a mother who was extremely attractive and only one year older than himself. They began a romance, and yet on camera, Alexander had to grow up in two successive scenes in his mother's company. As a boy, he first defended his father to his mother; then he had to defend his mother back to his father. After his father's murder he confronts his mother in an intense scene: during the takes, Colin heard Oliver, ten metres away, saying "Remember, this is the last time you'll ever see her." Olympias and Alexander, invisible to camera, were not planning such a thing in real life.

Romance was as nothing to the necessary explosions of emotion. At Philip's wedding, Colin had actually thrown his (rubber) cup at the head of the insolent Attalus: Attalus had the 'grace of a rhinoceros', he told me. In the family quarrels, he found himself drawing on his own memories of a past which had split his own family, the turbulent family holidays presided over by his father or the moments as a thirteen-year old boy when he found himself advising his own mother. He felt deeply that the roots of Alexander's ferocious genius had been formed in Macedonia. Between Macedonians and other Greeks, he saw not so much a conflict between cultures as one between classes, with other Greeks looking down on these wild northerners, like English looking down on the Irish. To underline the conflict, Oliver had cleverly opted for Irish and Celtic accents for his Macedonian stars. If Greeks like Aristotle were thought of as speaking 'king's English' from the centre of an old culture, the Macedonians would be clearly placed on the fringes by their Celtic voices. It might seem an easy choice for Colin who was born an Irishman, but the years in Hollywood had superimposed an American accent on him. He had to work hard to recover his original intonation. In the emotional scenes, there was the constant anxiety that it would slip.

"Was Alexander ever happy as king?", Colin asked me, "he was young, but I see him always with an old soul... if he was happy, it was never because of the plunder or what he could take for himself... perhaps he was happy, visiting Homer's Troy, perhaps on entering Babylon, but otherwise, maybe never... when Hephaestion is dying, he talks in the film as if the myth they have shared is over... there was an inner shame in him too after the tough march home through the desert". "What do you think Homer and Achilles meant to him?", I wondered, reverting to a major theme of my book. "If there had been no Achilles, he would still have behaved like Achilles," Colin answered. "Macedonia formed him, not Homer: there was no romance up at Pella. But Achilles was useful to him: "if you think I'm crazy", he could say, "then look at Achilles". He could use Achilles to present himself, especially when he was not strong enough to be his own man". I began to feel I should have talked more to this film-Alexander before writing my history.

In three consecutive weeks of filming Colin had to murder his officer Cleitus (Gary Stretch), receive the news of his beloved Hephaestion's death (Jared Leto) and then die himself in bed. The worst was murdering Gary. After a full day of retakes, finishing at 9pm, Colin sat for an hour in costume, and neither Claudine nor his trusted dresser, Tom, could coax him out of the role. He kept going over what he had done, while staring at his trailer's floor. Oliver had been delighted with the shots: "you're a genius, Farrell", he told him at the end, "but it comes at a price". The price was an inability to detach himself. Alexander, too, had been seized by dreadful remorse for the act which nowadays would have put him behind prison bars. On screen, Colin had acted with such force that he had even driven his spear through Gary Stretch's body armour and drawn blood. To prepare for the following scenes of remorse, Colin insisted on sleeping the night on the floor of the Indian palace set. He then had to act out the impact of Hephaestion's death and attack his wife, Roxane, on hearing news of it. What did he think Hephaestion meant to Alexander? "Inseparable friendship, above all: they were like brothers from different mothers. If sex happened when they were young, it was only an expression of something much greater... Hephaestion was the one who would judge him for what he was... the one to whom he had to prove himself..." And Roxane? "She was wild, yes, and the outsider – but she had a look of Olympias about her. Running subconsciously from his mother, Alexander was drawn to the same image: he then found this woman to be even more destructive... Or that's how Oliver has given the script such force. Alexander is caught subconsciously between the two, with nowhere left in the middle."

By mid-December, the strain was intense. "If you weren't Alexander", I asked him during a break, "who would you want to be?" "Diogenes", Colin answered, choosing the naked philosopher in his tub who wanted nothing, except that Alexander should stand aside and not block the sun. Did he know that in antiquity, people had credited Alexander himself with exactly this choice of alternative? Colin was aware that his role now set him apart from the other actors: they might share drinks afterwards but inside, he felt lonely and isolated. After his death, Alexander (Colin felt) knew a similar loneliness, the 'loneliness of power' in Harvard historian Ernst Badian's famous phrase about him. "Your book's not right, Robin," Colin told me, "you argue that in fact, Alexander was still surrounded by friends and drinking-companions and was not lonely at all. Believe me, you can be lonely, even with people around you..." It was now time for Colin to act out Alexander's death. Did he think, as some do, that Alexander was now a broken man who had lost sight of reality? "We don't know... maybe Oliver thinks he knows... Hephaestion was his real loss, his link, too, with honesty. For Alexander, change always seemed beautiful, and staying the same was dull. But did he still have strength?" Did Colin indeed, dying as if "nailed to a bed" which sloped awkwardly to help the camera-angle, while his Macedonians, like disciples, trooped passed him, with an ambivalent look from the 'Judas' who hated him, Cassander (Jonathan Rhys Meyers)? The days became longer and longer, often finishing at midnight or in the chilly small hours of the big unheated Babylon set. Colin hoped to die finally in five days before Christmas. But even then, more shots of the march-past turned out to be needed when filming restarted in the New Year and he had to be back for them.

Over Christmas, while not yet dead, Colin took himself off on an archaeological tour. He visited the pyramids in Egypt, re-meeting his film-mother Olympias: the star magazines were delighted, and the 'body language analysts' were sure there was still romance there, to "judge from the way Colin leans forward, trying to take something from her". Gossip raises a film's profile, but it was strictly on his own that Colin then went to Macedonia. Here were the real sites of Alexander's youth: the royal town of Pella and its mosaics, the theatre and palace at Vergina, the true site of Philip's murder, and the superb museum at Thessaloniki where the treasures of the Royal tombs, including what is surely Philip's own, are now displayed. For Colin, it was almost as emotional as acting all over again. He sat before Philip's ceremonial shield, his decorated breastplate and silver drinking cups and found himself talking to them, to the museum-attendants' surprise. "I've had to become what you never dared to be," he found himself saying to his father's relics. Fiction and reality became blurred in front of the greatest recent finds in the archaeology of Greece.

In Thailand, he had two big scenes left: the fall from Bucephalas in battle and then, up country on Thailand's borders with Laos, his speech to his reluctant army and his enforced decision to return home. Oliver had left the filming of this 'going home' scene to the last day of the schedule: by then, every single person on set would be echoing Colin's words of retreat. But would he ever get through them? "I don't sleep any more", he told me, "I get three hours a night, if I'm lucky: I have none of the reminders that I'm mortal. When I was young, it was so often the same. My father would tell me, "Colin, you're destined to be a night-watchman..." How ever should he play this final day? He was dreading it: "First, I have to show the troops I'm alive and still standing: but haven't I already had some of the mutineers taken off and killed? If so, I have turned myself into a tyrant... I have to run two bits of history into one". Does Oliver guide you much on set? I asked. "Usually, he tells me to do the first 'take' in my way – we've discussed it for months already – and only then – and I appreciate this – does he come back at me with so many ways to improve it". What is he like, then, with his script? "Half the time, you'd think he was Alexander himself... Alexander, but with a big dowsing of Dionysus..."

I suggested that, as Alexander first walks on alive after his wounding, he might think of Marlon Brando and of the epic last scenes of 'On the Waterfront' where a battered Brando manages to walk through the crowd of watching dockworkers. Perhaps it was an omen, perhaps Colin really was beginning to shadow his hero. The preceding scenes in the elephant battle had required him to rear up on Bucephalas in front of the war-elephants and to fall off the horse, wounded. On the first day, Colin pulled on the bridle of his black horse once too often and rearing up, the horse fell over backwards, every rider's nightmare. It crashed on the ground, only just missing the leg of the fallen Alexander. "I was too tired," Colin told me that evening, "to waste time on a small rearing-up: it nearly finished us". On the following days, he began by refusing to give way to a riding double and so he took the first falls in single combat himself. By the evenings, when we re-met, he had already followed a long day's work with a work-out in the hotel gym, trying to strengthen up his leg muscles. They were holding up, but only just.

On the final location, up country at Ubon Ratchathani, he fell again, twisting his foot in the hotel grounds, and realised, in agony, that this time, he had fractured an ankle. If he could only haul himself out on set, he really would be 'walking wounded', like Alexander himself at that moment. But the fracture had to be set and the health team were talking of six to eight weeks' minimum of rest. Despairing producers were resigned to an insurance claim and a costly return for the entire travelling circus in two months time. By flying Colin down to Bangkok, they could at least have him fitted with a plaster-cast: if the Thai doctors were willing to try a soft cast on the fracture, could the scene perhaps be finished with a real, authentic 'wound'? A soft cast was indeed fitted, and Colin returned to an 'army' on set who were almost as anxious, now, as Alexander's own. The props department ran up a pair of crutches: Perdiccas (Neil Jackson) already had knee-damage and could limp authentically beside him: if he could just walk the last 50 yards... Brando had never had such a preparation for his final, memorable stagger. Oliver has a favourite saying: "Adversity is an ally". At the last hurdle it was proving correct. The costume team had even borrowed a boot from the towering figure of Craterus (Rory McCann) whose feet are so enormous that with cutting, the boot could fit round Colin's leg, plaster-cast and all. Limping and fighting back the pain, 'Alexander' then made the most realistic 'return from the dead' in film history.

On the flight down to Bangkok, Thomas Schühly had decided that Colin must leave the airport by a private V.I.P. exit, to avoid any press attention or random photographs. At the desk, an uncertain Thai official had even asked, "who is this Colin Farrell? Why is he important?" "It's only my off-stage name," Colin answered mischievously, "I'm really Brad Pitt", "Ah", said the official, "Brad Pitt... this way, please; sign this paper as an autograph". So, Colin signed as Brad Pitt and left by the V.I.P. Door. After 'Alexander's' screening, he will need only to sign as himself in future. No other film-actor of his age could have played such a range at such a pitch or held an entire team for months in such commitment behind him. Even before his final, fatal role-play, I asked him what he made of it all. "I'd give it all up now," he answered, "just for one thing... to spend five minutes with Alexander himself".

Alexander (Colin Farrell) dressed in a more Oriental style in the Bactrian Fort.

Unit publicist Michael Singer, producer Moritz Borman and director Oliver Stone inspect some production photos on the Gaugamela battlefield.

Achilles in the Pella cave painting, wounded in the heel his mother had forgotten to bathe and protect.

6. Fixing The Funding

The film had a script and a promising star, but it still needed a cast and some serious money. By autumn 2002, buyers and bankers had to begin to stand forward. It was for Moritz Borman to find them, and the more the rival films were publicized, the harder his task became. It was already three years since Oliver's 'Any Given Sunday' . He had flourished in controversy throughout the 1990's; was he really to be trusted with a vast international epic?

Moritz found himself invited up to lunch with rival producer Dino di Laurentiis at Belle Aire in Beverly Hills. As always there was a friendly welcome and an excellent lunch: Dino talked of their respective costume- and set-drawings and even wondered if Moritz would like to read his script. In its August version it was based on the recent Alexander novel by Valerio Manfredi, one of Oliver and Thomas's initial helpers ten years before. Historically, it was distorted (Alexander's first mistress dies at Gaugamela, twenty years too soon): there were soppy scenes with Alexander's dog, a series of staged set-pieces, a completely unhistorical beginning among the slaves at Philip's gold-mines, one of whom Alexander saved, and an abrupt ending in India without any of the drama of Alexander's return to Babylon. Dino had even been contemplating that Alexander should die in India on the battlefield so as to finish off the film. The sex-scenes were frightful, including a moment when Hephaestion returned to find Alexander in bed with a Greek concubine; he flexed his muscles before joining them in a threesome.

To put it mildly, Dino needed a script and over coffee he tried to secure one. "Who owns Oliver Stone's script?", he asked. "We've bought it", Moritz told him. "So - why not bring Oliver's good script to us and we will get Baz Luhrmann to make it?" In Moritz's view, a film, for Dino, is just a commodity. Personally, he had staked his faith on Oliver as writer, director and friend: Dino's bid made him even more determined to succeed.

Just under $11 million had been put up for pre-production expenses, but at least another $150 million would be needed to see it all to completion. The sums sound huge, but they are less than the cost of Terminator III (c. $213 million) or a few years ago, Titanic (c. $210 million). The producers and investors expect to agree a deal with distributors who will then guarantee big sums for publicity and for printing copies of the film. In the US alone, a film on Alexander's scale would expect at least $35 million to be spent on publicity, including trailers in cinemas and commercials on television, and the distribution of, say, 2500 copies of the film to cinemas, each costing up to $1500. Cinema-owners then take about half of the box-office takings. How can anyone ever make money? Films run for ever shorter periods on their first release, and three weeks in a city are exceptional. However, financiers work with a rough rule of thumb: total box-office gross takings should work out at about three times the takings of the film's all-important first weekend. Afterwards come the television rights, which can be a substantial income, and not only video rights but the recent significant 'extra' of DVD. In these DVD days, long runs in the cinema are becoming less important. Terminator III had pulled in $453 million, proving that big projects are rewarding, and the Californian trend has been towards big projects too.

The vital next step, for Moritz, was to be sure of meeting production costs. Intermedia with the IMF investors would put up another $45 million, but to bring them in, Moritz needed to start selling distribution rights in each country or group of territories. Big American distributors were sure to be keen, but which of the various 'Alexander' projects would they back? Moritz had sent the script to Paul Rassam, the respected director of France's Pathé films. Paul's experienced eye had liked it and understood it: he also resepected Oliver and verbally, in October 2002, he committed Pathé to a significant sum for the distribution rights in France. The offer was doubly important, for if Moritz could start to pre-sell foreign territories, then the investors in IMF would put their second, major sum into the film for its actual production.

Out in Thailand, while war-elephants were threatening the Macedonian phalanx, I sat with Paul Rassam and recalled his bold decision. Paul has known all the Hollywood 'greats' and stored his anecdotes about each one of them. Yes, he admired Oliver: back in 1983, it was Dino, no less, who had handed Paul a red-bound volume of script and asked him to read it to see if he should make it into a film or not. It was the script of 'Platoon': Paul told him to make it, because the script had such intensity. Notoriously, Dino then threw away his chance, after tieing Oliver to write a screenplay for his 'Year of the Dragon'. It took Oliver a lawsuit to reclaim his rights in 'Platoon', but it was Dino who lost the chance of an Oscar-winning film.

Under a tamarind tree in the lunch hour, Paul quoted to me Cicero in Latin and reflected how he wanted to make a film about the Roman republic. Was this unexpected love of classics a reason why he had backed 'Alexander'? "Look", he answered, "I gave up Latin when I was 18. I studied engineering and mathematics: the reason why I backed 'Alexander' is that I like Oliver and I like the script. When I started reading, it had a great beginning: 'To whom, Alexander...?' on his deathbed. It cannot include everything: it is not a totality, but it has such scope. It is not a usual film. It is a film, in the end, about suffering..." Had it been a difficult decision? "No, but it was made difficult. Late in 2002, Dino asked me round to meet him in New York in a suite in the Plaza Atheneé hotel. 'Paul', he told me, 'you can have the right to distribute my own Alexander film in France for next to nothing - just give up on Oliver.' And he said there was someone who had just arrived who would like to meet us both next door. He opened the door: there was Baz Luhrmann." And what did you do? "I went back to Moritz and signed the deal we had agreed. But Dino was jealous. Even in the summer, in Venice, he kept telling me, 'You're the only one of my friends who's against me'". One of Paul's ancestors is famous to scholars for excavating Assyrian palaces and giving his name to an ancient clay-cylinder, found in Iraq, not far from the site of the Gaugamela battle. In the latest French handbook on Babylon, this Hormuzed Rassam of the 1850's is described as 'more of a pirate than an archaeologist'. But Paul had stayed loyal.

For Moritz, December 2002 was a golden month. Warner Brothers had distributed five of Oliver's films and Moritz found himself invited to the offices of Alan Horn, Warner Brothers' president. "Oliver is one of the most brilliant film-makers we have", Alan told him, "so I will do it. We'll buy Alexander in the US." The price still had to be fixed and Warners might want other territories included. But at last, the gamble was a reality.

Distributors promise payments which will be made on delivery of the film. For the weeks between the start and the end of filming, film-makers have to turn to the banks and agree a Completion Bond, payable in stages before the picture is completed. The terms vary according to the risk of the project, the director and the location: Morocco, Oliver Stone and Alexander in battle were never going to be the easiest deal. In February 2003, two additional producers were signed up to pull things together: Jon Kilik, from New York, and as Jon had not done a really big film before, Scotsman Iain Smith who had worked in Morocco and had been part of the team for 'Chariots of Fire'. Two crucial calculations now became real: the film schedule and the foreign currency factor. Both these decisions proved vital. The shooting schedule would be very tight (on 'Troy', Wolfgang Petersen had been given 110-120 days) but Oliver is famously efficient with a schedule: 'Alexander' would eventually be done in 95 days. At that rate, Iain Smith calculated, each day on an outdoor location would cost 260,000 dollars in fixed costs. The dollar was equally important. Before filming, it was hedged at 1.60 to the pound and by the end, it had fallen to 1.86, a loss of more than 15%. If the producers and financiers had got the dollar wrong, the film would have been seriously impeded.

The unpredictable problem was the film's competitor. Even without a final script, Dino's team were publicizing their intentions to start their film at once, whereas Moritz's project had a script (they were saying) that was supposedly full of drugs, vice and sex. In fact, the sex-scenes were in Dino's script and were far more explicit.

At the Cannes' film festival in May 2003, Moritz hoped to sell the remaining foreign territories. France, Germany and England offer tax-remissions to local investors and film-makers in order to encourage their national film industries. Oliver has a French mother and has lived in Paris: in early 2003 his French citizenship had been revived, with important financial benfits for the film. In England, the sets would be built in Pinewood and Shepperton, attracting further financial support. The script already had a German and an English input; Alexander himself was Irish: the production was to be a co-production in France and England, with France providing both the excellent sound-team and most of the 'visual effects' in post-production. What the newspapers were wrongly calling a 'Hollywood sword-and-sandals epic' was not a purely 'Hollywood' film. The characters used spears and sarissas and wore boots, not sandals, anyway.

For two days out in Cannes, Moritz needed Oliver to concentrate in a small office-room, while companies from all over the film-world came and asked them about the remaining 'Alexander' rights. Only once did Oliver drop guard, when a German potential buyer used his fifteen-minute appointment to ask about 'Alexander's' rumoured sex-scenes. "Of course, they'll be having sex all the over the set", Oliver misled him. "No, Oliver", Moritz answered, "it will not be like that at all." The next morning, the German rang up and declined to bid for the rights: it was not that he was worried about the sex, he told Moritz, but he was worried that the film's financier should already be disagreeing with the director and telling him what to do.

Back in England, newspapers were talking only of Dino and saying that Oliver's 'rival' project was in trouble in 'terrorist-prone' Morocco. It was pure manipulation, but the result, as intended, was to squeeze Moritz's options. In the face of Dino's publicity, Japan, England and Italy were territories which proved particularly hard to sell. Naturally, Warner Brothers struck an increasingly hard bargain for their own areas, while the banks were only too ready to impose tougher terms. Six weeks before filming, with these territories in the balance, the production was still short of its projected needs of $150 million and the banks had yet to finalize a full Completion Bond. If the end was uncertain, why risk the beginning? Smith and Kilik were needing money urgently for stars, sets and costumes and as everything had to be bought, a delay would ruin the entire schedule. "Why are you not sending the money over?", they telephoned to Moritz. "Because I haven't got it."

One way was to give up, but Alexander himself never took that way: he ran the risk. Heroically, Moritz managed to persuade Time Warner to advance monies due from the success of 'Terminator III', a film backed by IMF investors. These funds reached IMF's 'collection account' and could be switched immediately to Alexander's needs. But even when filming began in Morocco, the oustanding territories were still unsold. Japanese buyers had to come to Marrakesh and watch the first film-cut of dust-clouds from our cavalry charging through the desert. In the end, it was irresistible. In November, even Japan was sold and 'Alexander' was assured of a world-wide distribution.

"Remember", Paul Rassam told me, "we were being told to invest in a film whose director is a rebellious American, whose star is a wild Irishman and whose cameraman is a crazy Mexican. But there is one other thing - they're all geniuses." In early December, on the Babylon set at Pinewood, the word then spread that it was Dino's film which had to be abandoned. The race had gone to the straightest runner. "Dino's project is dead", Thomas Schühly assured me, "and believe me, there will be no Easter."

The interior Hall of the Babylon Palace built in Pinewood.

7. CASTING AROUND

While the film's financing was being fixed in Europe and America, Oliver and his agents were engaged on a trail which is just as difficult: casting. 'Alexander' would be the making of many careers. The script had come to have an excellent range of parts, from Aristotle to the eunuch Bagoas. Colin was fixed at the centre, but who would be right for the film's backbone, the elderly Ptolemy, and for the two Macedonian pillars, Philip and Olympias? In Oliver's mind, old Ptolemy had been cast from an early date as Anthony Hopkins. The two of them had worked on 'Nixon' and were well used to each other's ways. There would be difficulties over Hopkins' availability, but as the narrator, much of his part could be filmed in one compressed stretch of time. "Hopkins approaches a scene", Oliver later told me in London, "like a dog with a bone. He circles round it, he worries at it and then he bites into it and hits the level he wants. What is then so striking is that he keeps that same level up for take after take. The others zig-zag, up and down. On one take, they hit it, the next they lose it again." Onlookers were startled when Oliver went up to the great man on the Alexandria balcony in Pinewood and asked him audibly, after the first shot, "Anthony, what's happened? Is something wrong, or have you lost it since you moved away from England? What are we to do about it?" A needled Hopkins drew back, just as Oliver intended, and proceeded to hit the highest level for shot after shot without faltering. In mid-December, the Shepperton days became almost impossibly long, lasting well past midnight and once, until nearly 3 in the morning. The next day was a Saturday, but in a very tight schedule, Anthony Hopkins had to be back on set to do long stretches of his narrator's 'voice-over'. He began on the dot at midday and continued, without faltering, until early evening. Even Oliver's stamina had been tested, although, as he concluded, "we managed to coax out of him some of the best of that Welsh intonation from his early years." It was a stunning show of professionalism, greeted by applause and cries of 'Why do we bother?' from the young supporting actors when they later saw the uncut footage in a dark hotel-room in Bangkok.

We know King Ptolemy's distinctive features from portraits on his silver coins: Hopkins' nose, in particular, needed careful make-up. But if he was the very old Ptolemy, who on earth could play young Ptolemy? There would also have to be a young Alexander (where Connor Paolo eventually gave a performance of almost unnerving cool and self-assurance) and in Oliver's mind, there should be a resemblance between Alexander's mother Olympias and his eventual bride, Roxane. Before casting one of them, the other would have to be fixed. It was no use asking me: Harrison Ford as Philip and Catherine Zeta Jones as Olympias? Or Ralph Fiennes, perhaps, with Meryl Streep in one of her wilder moods? We have no idea of the historical Olympias's looks, although the bearded Philip is known from portraits on his silver coins, from a recently-found hunting-scene painted on the outside of his tomb at Vergina and from a small ivory head from the funerary couch inside it. His face, even, has been reconstructed form the cremated bones found in its casket. Not until June did Oliver decide on Angelina Jolie, with Val Kilmer joining the cast soon afterwards. In 2001, Oliver had been working on a romantic story, 'Beyond Borders', in which Angelina was to have played. As Olympias, she would be so close in age to Colin that it would be hard at first to see her as his mother. But in Greece, her casting would be very popular, as she had left such good memories of her days on the island of Santorini in her recent role as Lara Croft.

Oliver had various agents helping him, especially Billy Hopkins in New York and up and coming Lucinda Sysons in Covent Garden, London. Colin's Irish presence at the centre encouraged Oliver and Lucinda to look to Ireland in order to cast the supporting officers. With the help of Rebecca Roper in Dublin, tapes would be recorded by a selection of possible actors either in Dublin or in Lucinda's third-floor London office and sent on to Oliver and Billy Hopkins in the U.S.A. From these possibles, a cast was selected for auditioning in Oliver's presence. Lucinda's aim throughout is to keep options open while working with the Director's general guidance: nobody was fixed too quickly into one particular role. In Oliver, she found a director with an unusually sharp eye and an emotional sense of what he wanted, guided by his heart and the 'right feel'. In Dublin, therefore, forty actors were gathered just for the first day of Oliver's auditioning. Rebecca Roper would act a dialogue part and Oliver would sit listening, wearing his hallmark red sports shirt with an open neck and a pair of headphones, just like one of the football commentators, Lucinda thought, in his 'Any Given Sunday'. It was still entirely open which actor might be cast for exactly which part, but Oliver wanted a cohesive team who could bond round Colin, accept a physically rigorous training and carry morale right through to the concluding scenes of 'mutiny'. Even he cannot have hoped for the team spirit which resulted. Ian Beattie (Antigonus), Denis Conway (Nearchus), Garrett Lombard (Leonnatus), Jonathan Rhys Meyers (Cassander) and John Kavanagh (Parmenion) were among those who brought an Irish open-heartedness and camaraderie to a screenplay which exposed them to heat, discomfort and bursts of intense physical action. In Thailand, even after 80 days' filming, it took little to persuade them to break into Irish songs ('Molly Malone') while their phalanx-units were regrouping for another stand against the elephants.

Individual auditions were for fifteen minutes maximum, except when Denis Conway delighted Oliver by performing Shakespeare from memory, including extracts from his favourite, Richard III. For Elliot Cowan (young Ptolemy) it was a marked change from his previous auditioning, all of it for theatre-parts. Fresh from Chekhov's 'The Seagull' with Fiona Shaw in Edinburgh, he found himself in Kensington's Royal Garden Hotel with ten others, picking out parts from the different scripts before them. After a recent role in Oxford, he happened to arrive holding a copy of my Alexander-book (a point, he kindly

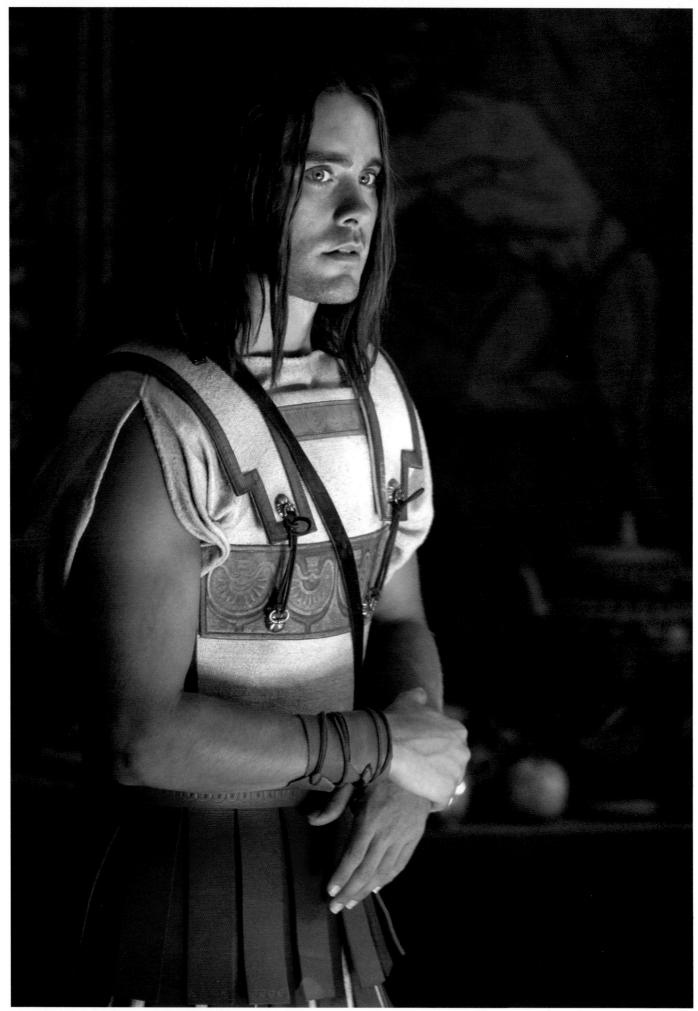

Loyal Hephaestion (Jared Leto) admires Alexander in the campaign tent before Gaugamela.

Queen Olympias (Angelina Jolie) as time passes during her son Alexander's absence in the East.

believes, which counted in his favour) and when he found himself having to improvise, his theatrical background came into its own. Oliver relished the improvisations. "Why doesn't Britain know about him?", Oliver asked a pleased Lucinda who had spotted Elliot while casting for Troy. Elliot still had no idea which part he might be given, but Oliver had noticed how his eyes, nose and features had a definite look of a young Anthony Hopkins. Elliot's mother is an ardent Hopkins-fan and would have been thrilled to know of the resemblance. "He looks awesome in a plumed helmet", Oliver remarked, and a day later, he confirmed Elliot as Hopkins' young 'other self'. He would not meet his older half until November 15, well into filming, at London's Charlotte Street Hotel. He was impressed by Hopkins's big physical presence and his strong handshake. "A striking resemblance", Sir Anthony commented, and together, they reflected on their shared English R.A.D.A. experience, its favoured 'Laban Technique' and its principle of involving each actor in his character.

Out in New York, Jared Leto found himself part of another crowd of hopefuls. "It was two years", he recalled for me, "since I last auditioned, and the crowd was more like a cattle-market than a Greek chorus. Fifty of us were swarming in, so I checked my ego at the door and reckoned I had nothing to hide..." Inside, he found himself on trial as Hephaestion, Alexander's most intimate friend since boyhood. Jared understood very well that although their friendship was surely a homoerotic one, it was stronger and broader than a sexual romance. The "sex", he reckoned, "was a footnote." A homosexual, one-way orientation would strike the wrong note, so "I played it as if we were brothers, born from different mothers," Colin's way of seeing it too. During his audition, one of the casting directors lay with his head in Jared's lap, reading Alexander's part, until Jared almost found himself breaking into laughter: here he was, playing Alexander's great 'boyfriend', with a black-haired New Yorker facing sideways across his knee. What if the man was gay? In Jared's view, "90% of my audition was nervous nonsense", but Oliver saw the potential, and Jared joined the cast with the brief to 'love Colin loyally'. It was not too difficult, as he already respected Colin for his performance in 'Phone Booth'. Near the end of filming, the two of them even exchanged locks of hair as mementoes for the medallions they wear round their necks.

In June, Oliver flew into Dublin for a script rehearsal with the actors cast so far. Lucinda arrived to meet him, carrying so many copies of a top-secret script in one big suitcase that she felt in need of a security guard. Oliver was nervous, but as they walked round the building, he revealed that Angelina was now settled in his mind as Olympias: even Lucinda could not quite imagine the brilliant mixture of passion, cool detachment and persuasive psychosis which Angelina then brought out of the part. The two of them then went in, and spent a long day reading through the parts in the first-ever group meeting. Colin was in commanding form, but Lucinda was intrigued to see a casting on whom Oliver had insisted, Gary Stretch as Cleitus the Macedonian veteran. Gary is best known as a professional boxing champion, with only one small film-part behind him, but he and Oliver had met up in Thailand during the previous autumn and Oliver had ended their intense encounter by offering Gary the film-part of the officer Cleitus whom Alexander murders. When we met on the desert-set in Morocco, Gary asked me, as Cleitus, "what am I really like?" I told him to remember that Cleitus surely never read a book. "Nor have I", said Gary thankfully, and surprised my nearby cavalrymen by giving me a kiss. In Hopkins's absence, Oliver read for the elder Ptolemy, with a force which impressed his fellow-actors. By mid-afternoon, matters became suitably heated: it was for Colin to insult Gary and then murder him and in the emotion of the moment, furniture began to fall around in the rehearsal-room. The same emotion would re-surface at Pinewood in November when Gary rose to the challenge and made a powerful response to Colin's rage in one of the most intense scenes in the film.

If Angelina was to be Olympias, who ever could be Roxane? As the script had progressed, Roxane had emerged as a turning point, far from the tall and elegant 'Amazon' whom Thomas Schühly had once envisaged. Oliver still wanted her to have a look of Olympias, and co-producer Jon Kilik remembered the impression left on him by a young New York actress, Rosario Dawson. She had played in Spike Lee's emotional '25th Hour' and in action-adventures such as 'Welcome to the Jungle', but an ancient Bactrian was something else. From tapes and photos Oliver was still uncertain, but an audition in New York convinced him that he had found someone quite different to the crowd. Aged 24, Rosario describes herself as a 'race-mixture on two legs', combining Puerto-Rican, Cuban, Afro-American and even a relevant dash of Irish. She was brought up in a squat in Manhattan's Lower East Side and began her film career 'for fun' aged 15. There was height in her family (her mother is 6 feet, her brother 6"5), but Rosario, no single-breasted Amazon, brought an exceptional energy and quick-wittedness. She would never make an Alexander 'impotent', as Thomas Schühly's script-comments had once feared. Her audition was not far gone before Oliver was already calling her 'Roxane' and commenting on her look of Angelina. She left, "making 295 calls on my mobile", knowing she had pulled off the coup. She did have to learn a dance-routine which choreographer Piers Gielgud was basing on East Iranian dance-steps. Until then, clubbing had been more her line, combined with the ambition to be a basketball star. But she is fit and on for anything: in the summer, she runs with the bulls in the bull-ring at Pamplona.

On set in Pinewood, Rosario would find herself clapped into a heavy costume and a face veil and left waiting until Colin was ready to start their wedding-night. Star photographer Robert Maxwell took shots of her under hot lights whereupon Rosario fainted in the heat under her heavy clothing. "And what on earth did you do next?", I asked her. "When I recovered, that's when I started slapping him." Slapping Colin? Until then she had followed the scripting for her introduction to her husband, but Oliver was finding it all too tame. So Rosario suggested that first she should slap Colin and then set about him with a knife. Her slapping was so effective that it brought out old bruises from 'Daredevil' round Colin's eye. "A knife, Rosario?" Oliver asked: "could you not just fondle a snake?" "Sure, give me a knife: I have twenty of them back home", so they chose one coated in snake-skin: "shall I gut the snake with it for starters?" There is not much that a Puerto-Rican lady needs to learn about knife-handling, Rosario set about Colin all over again, nearly scaring even him until she showed that she knew how to keep the knife-point away from a man's throat by a neat flick with her thumb. After the violence, there had to be something sexual. The scripting said only: "Her back to us, she is now naked to him, her skin the colour of amber, Alexander wearing the expression of a conflicted textbook mythic hero" but somehow, it still seemed flat. "If we dilly-dally," Rosario told herself, "we'll be here all week". Makeup had painted black snakes coiling up her back and rear-view: why not show them to the camera? She had never gone further before than bare shoulders in a bubble-bath, but the set was firmly curtained off and as Oliver wondered quite what to ask her, she put him out of his anxiety: "What about a bare chest and hard nipples? Will they wake you up?" Was it awkward, I asked her: "no, because I was still acting and worrying about my lines, but I did think half way through, "God, the cameraman can see the snakes on my bum...". Cameraman Rodrigo reassures me that he was intent on his light-meter. After turning up the dramatic heat, Rosario left Colin to thrash around on a bed without her. Instead, she gave a phone call to her mum in New York. "And what did she say about it?" "Good on you, girl" – she was naked in the bath". And Rosario went back stage, put on her black-framed spectacles and returned to her favourite pastime on set: reading a classic novel.

In the script, Roxane feels and provokes jealousy from her rivals for Alexander's affections, Hephaestion and the eunuch Bagoas. "Roxane has a black heart", Jared Leto observed, but in real life Rosario and Bagoas were to strike up one of the production's closest friendships. It is not easy to cast a eunuch. From ancient evidence, we infer that Persian eunuchs were either castrated when pre-pubescent or when post-pubescent. Post-pubescent eunuchs would tend to be the fat ones, but young Bagoas should be pre-pubescent, light and agile. In Paris, Lucinda had hopes of a blonde candidate who was half-Moroccan, but when he did not come good at audition, she was reminded of someone right outside films: a young Spanish-born ballet dancer with the English National Ballet whom had been seen on tapes of a recent TV commercial. At the time, Francisco Bosch, aged 19, was about to go off to dance in Greece, expecting to be cast in 'Coppelia'. Lucinda sent for him and in a darkened room, Oliver told him, "seduce me...": Francisco, of course, danced beautifully and his dark-haired boyish look secured him the part. While choreographer Piers Gielgud easily taught him the un-classical dance-steps, the lines and acting were quite another matter. Francisco had to speak, then kiss Colin on the lips and retire with him under the bed-blankets. It was hard enough for him to remember his words under the lights, but despite having kissed Rosario for luck before going on set, he froze with Colin before him and had to be pushed wholeheartedly into it by Colin himself. "Just play it as skin and silence," Colin told him in their bed. A second-year dancer in a 'corps de ballet' is not a trained actor, but Francisco loved the team-spirit, the friendliness of the entire crew and the contrast with the jealousies of a professional dance-company in training. "I'll miss it so much," he told me as he left Thailand, "and all I'm going back to is a dancing-part with a waltz in Swan Lake".

One of the bigger pieces in Lucinda's casting puzzle was burly Macedonian veteran, Craterus. Here, she needed somebody physically imposing who could play the honest soldier, steadying the infantry line ("Fear is rot...") and speaking up for their wish to go home. An older Irish voice had already been found in John Kavanagh (Parmenion), uniquely capable, after his years of theatre, of being clearly heard above the clatter of battle on Gaugamela's left wing. So, for Craterus she looked north, to Scotland. In 2003, Rory McCann's film career was scarcely two years old. Six foot six inches tall, dark haired, and muscular, he had earned a living painting Scotland's Forth Bridge from the end of a rope. Before that, he had been a tree-surgeon, cutting out the dead wood of Scotland's forests with a chainsaw. Actually, the Macedonians themselves were famous foresters and little did Lucinda know that Rory's profession was exactly right for them: Craterus surely chopped logs in his youth. Acting took Rory away from forestry, starting him off in commercials. The parts which had made him a well-known face were firstly, one as a paraplegic hero in a wheelchair and then, as the muscular advertisement on the front of the packets of Scotland's beloved porridge-oats. A massive presence, he found his part doubled when actor Brian Blessed had to scale back after a temporary injury. It was for Rory, instead, to speak up with a strong accent and urge Alexander that his men must turn back from India. With a typical generosity, Val Kilmer (Philip) coached Rory through the set-piece line-by-line during a brief return to Thailand. On the battlefield Rory needed no coaching. As his army waited apprehensively for Hollywood's first-ever charge of elephants, Rory looked up from the front line and saw an even greater danger hanging above the troops' heads. Half of a tree's trunk had split and was hanging by a precarious branch: Craterus the forester called a halt and saved a possible catastrophe by his trained tree-surgeon's eye.

By mid-August, Oliver had his main cast, but there was still the need to match their voices into an agreed type of speech. In antiquity, Macedonians were known for their own dialect (it is now believed to be a form of north-west Greek) and when they spoke it, they would sound almost incomprehensible to the likes of Demosthenes in Athens: in Macedon, 'Philip' was pronounced more as 'Vilip'. Oliver decided to go for English with a regional accent: Welsh (Hopkins and Elliot), Scottish (Rory) and Irish for other main players, with educated voices like Aristotle representing the centrally 'received pronunciation'. The choice gave viewers the sense (shared by many in antiquity) of Macedonians with a northern Greek tone. To help to standardise it, Oliver chose as his Dialogue coach Catherine Charlton; Catherine is experienced from her work on film and in school rooms, where she has taught and recorded English as spoken abroad.

A Dialogue Coach is traditionally an actor's worst enemy. Day after day, Catherine would sit on set in headphones, checking the accent and delivery of every line spoken to camera. It was for her to rehearse each star and to teach them her 'Alexander technique' of breathing and voice-projection: if the abdomen is held in too tightly, the body will over-compensate with excessive tightness in the neck. Catherine has known actors who have greeted her, only half in jest, with crossed fingers, as if to keep off a vampire. It was a help, then, when Colin greeted her openly in Morocco and told the others, "I love her already". But friendliness did not make the job any easier. Oliver had chosen a strongly Irish supporting cast, but their regional Irish varied (Ian was from Belfast, Denis from Cork), and Colin's Irish had been superimposed by his years in California. For Jared Leto, the entire accent had to be learned from scratch. During the intense scenes of his death at Pinewood, Jared would pace the London streets after dark, declaiming lines to keep his Irish and his energy in place. During the Christmas break, he was so afraid that he would slip back into 'Californian' that he went to Ireland instead, playing tapes every night of the accent he had to retain.

Would Alexander's voice have changed as he aged and moved eastwards into each new culture? Oliver and Catherine decided it would not. Certainly, though, young Ptolemy (Elliot Cowan) would have to match the voice of Hopkins, but Hopkins would tend towards Welsh. As Hopkins was arriving only two thirds of the way through filming, Catherine and Elliot had to work from tapes of 'Remains of the Day' and hope that his voice had not altered since emigrating. In Morocco, Catherine's hotel room became the rendezvous for one actor after another, until she began to wonder what the management was thinking of her. There were voice-exercises to learn, tricks to master at the line-ends and a constant need to initiate the film-novices, Gary and Francisco. How, too, were non-Macedonians to speak? Olympias came from the Greek kingdom west of Macedon, and Oliver wanted her to be distinct from the Irish-Macedonian. Catherine turned to her tapes of schoolchildren learning English in north-western Greece and encouraged Angelina to speak more from the front of her mouth. Singing, however, was a new ordeal for her (Angelina did not even have the final words of her opening 'lullaby' to Alexander until two days before filming it). What about the Persians? They were now cast to include actors with a French natural accent or a touch of German-Turk (Bessus). Catherine consulted in each case with John Wells, specialist in phonetics at University College, London. He helped her with the problem words and intonations: the Persians ended up being modelled on Farsi-speakers who had learned English as a second language. On the desert-location in Morocco, I then recorded for Catherine every Greek-based word and name in an 'Oxford English' pronunciation; with only a few compromises, Americanisms like 'phay-lanx' were eliminated. Audiences expecting the usual Hollywood 'clangers' will be surprised by this absence. It was a struggle to work it through, and as intense training began, Catherine's mother died in England. She flew back for a few days' break, returning to find that Val Kilmer, her most high-spirited 'client', had filled her room with white roses in appreciation.

In Val Kilmer's view, Oliver 'is never bound by reality'. Naturally, there were still gaps for last minute castings, for children and wine-pourers at the Bactrian wedding or for yet more Macedonian veterans. Oliver's own family found themselves pitched into the wedding-scenes with publicist Michael Singer as a wine-pourer and Rodrigo's enchanting young children as onlookers, one of whom, Ximena, has ambitions anyway to be an actress. In Pinewood, Oliver also rounded up old age pensioners from English casting-lists to serve in 'India' as Alexander's veteran Shield-bearers. Quite undaunted, the pensioners were to be found in Thailand, eating breakfast in their armour at 6 am, at ages ranging up to Stanley at 72, survivor of a heart by-pass but fit enough for a day in the ranks against elephants in a heat of 40°C. Nonetheless, in Morocco Oliver still needed two more old Macedonians, the respected Antipater (who would supervise Greece in Alexander's absence) and his successor as regent, Polyperchon. While driving across the desert in a jeep, Oliver shouted to script-supervisor Sue Field to stop at once: "There's Polyperchon", he called at the unsuspecting Chris Aberdien who was emerging, aged 64, from the lunch tent. "Be a general, Chris". "I'd be honoured, sir", and so each day in body-armour Chris served Macedonia, reserving his one line for the council in Bactria where he spoke, to general applause, for the 'honour of the kingdom'. It was left, then, to Sue to come up with a non-speaking Antipater. "I don't want to see you", Oliver told her, "until you've found one; just bring me one, the right guy." So she brought on Cyril Gibbons, the production's Health and Safety Officer. Who better to uphold Macedonian security in Alexander's absence?

Roxane (Rosario Dawson) with Hephaestion (Jared Leto) of whom she is so jealous.

8. SETTING IT UP

Alexander's career was one of constant movement, taking him to the world's oldest and greatest cities, Tyre, Gaza, Memphis in Egypt, Babylon, Susa. He also broke into what for Greeks was a new world, north-western India with its wise men, elephants and snakes. In the 1970's, plans for an Alexander film had always foundered on the number and scale of the film sites it would require. Since the 1980's, some of these sites could be simulated or enlarged by computer graphics: grandeur has become cheaper and more attainable. But the actors still need sets and the 'look' of the film needs a central core of locations. In Oliver's mind, they must each have a distinctive 'look' and a different light, to back up his web of inter-relating stories. A historian like myself would come to realise that 'look' and 'light' are the elusive qualities which make or (supposedly) break a film. Producers will give them vast sums from their budgets, while research by trained historians deserves-nothing of the sort.

As the script drafts settled down, the locations became clearer. Until Stone Draft 4 (April 2003) the desert oracle at Siwah was one of them. Persepolis, the great Persian palace-complex, was still a possibility, if only so that Alexander could burn it down. So was the huge funeral pyre which Alexander built for Hephaestion in Babylon and planned to burn down too: Oliver particularly regretted that expense obliged him to cut this scene out. The 'look ' of all these locations would be the responsibility of a Production Designer who would be subject to Oliver's veto. From 2002 onwards, Oliver had his man, the inexhaustible Jan Roelfs.

Jan had begun his career as an architect in Holland. In films, he had been acclaimed for his work with director Peter Greenaway; he had designed 'Little Women'; he was famous for his design of the fantasy sets and Elizabethan splendour for 'Orlando' and most recently for the futurist vision for 'Gattaca'.

On 'Alexander' he faced an even greater challenge. The sets divide into 'outdoors' and 'indoors': it was his responsibility to find suitable outdoor locations, places with the right light. It was also his responsibility to draw every building which would be used outdoors and indoors, and to preside over the detailed 'look' which their decoration would give them. Ancient history had never been part of his career or training, but he would have to envisage many thousands more ancient buildings, art objects and fabrics than most archaeology-departments in a university can study in a lifetime. Whole cities would have to appear in the views around whatever he chose to construct. Roelfs and his team would draw them all and send them off to 'visual effects' specialists who would simulate them on computers and add them into the film's background.

Outside his film-work, Roelfs is a true 'flying Dutchman', dividing his life between Holland, New York and Japan. For Oliver, he would preside, nonetheless, over a tightly run budget, sensibly pitched for the maximum 'low' cost effect: his strength here was crucial to his selection. The indoor sets were quickly located. Since 1997, the British government has been offering tax-breaks for film productions in England, and so Pinewood and Shepperton studios were the obvious financial choices.

Outdoors, where should 'Alexander's' travelling hordes settle? In Greece, sites like Philip's theatre and the town of Pella have been partly excavated by archaeologists. However, there was no question ever of filming at or near their remains. The 'illusion of reality' does not depend on reality. Ruins would only get in the way of it, and if a site was blocked up with trenches and tourists it would be completely unsuitable for filming. Before the film, none of these sites was even visited. Instead, during 2001 and 2002, scouting-parties kept circulating from one possible country to another, sending for Jan and sometimes attracting Oliver too. For a while, the coast and mountains of Spain headed the list, with Tunisia, Morocco, then Malta even, and India and finally Thailand in support: except for India, not one of these countries had been visited by Alexander himself. Oliver and Jan had agreed very quickly on the sort of scenery which each section needed. Macedonia should be bright and sunny with a blue sea in or near the picture to emphasise that we were in Greece, beside the Aegean: the Bactrian fort must be in or near steep cliffs and mountains; the battle with the elephants in India must have a distinctive light and a combination of forest-tones and vivid green jungle: when the army turns back in India, the view to the distance must be Oriental, with rivers and a never-ending prospect. Malta came onto the list because it had a good Meditarranean feel and the ever-present sea: the harbours were good and the blue sky proved to be useful on stills and plates for visual effects. Tunisia was a strong contender, as it had a variety which could house several scenes at once. There was even an idea of filming the entire Gaugamela battle in California and relying on computer graphics only. Fortunately for us cavalrymen, the cost was impossibly high.

By 2002, the choices were still unresolved. It sounds absurd to outsiders, but insiders know all the elements which come into the reckoning. The chosen site must be accessible; if possible, a single country should be varied enough to satisfy several types of different location, thereby saving on transport; there must be housing for a big film-crew, usable roads and political stability. There must also be a supply of affordable extras for the crowds and armies, preferably a tradition of film-making and a supporting range of crafts and materials at prices which 'Alexander's' budget could afford. For a while, three separate 'Alexanders' were threatening to invade the Mediterranean at the same time. The HBO series was planning to build Pella in Italy, about an hour's journey from Rome: Italy, they felt, would be more attractive to the actors than Spain. Di Laurentiis was talking of a major presence in Morocco: Jan and Oliver were flying to and fro, wondering about Spain or Malta or Morocco, too, and India.

When the financing became more stable in early 2003, the options had to crystallize. Morocco had the variety and could even take the desert battle, Macedonia-by-the-sea, the Bactrian fort in the mountains, the entry gate to Babylon and some jungle, if necessary. For five days, Jan surveyed the country from a helicopter, checking out the sites which his scouts on the ground had recommended. There was no real problem with the local back-up. Moroccan craftsmen and workshops are thoroughly familiar with the speed and demands of a big film production. They can turn out window-screens, carpeting or bits of armour by the hundred, while they know every trick with mud-brick walling. The Moroccan army, too, would assign soldiers and conscripts for any sort of battle. The problems, rather, were atmospheric. If the look of each section was to vary, the light had to vary with it. The Moroccan deserts would be sharply lit from a pale sky for most of the day, but could the light for a jungle battle really be distinct enough? What was missing was a boundless 'Indian' view for the scene of the army's turning-back. There was also a serious animal problem: Morocco could not provide elephants. Thomas Schühly even explored an elephant-trainer in Thailand who was offering to ship elephants and their keepers by sea to Morocco: would it be cheaper and safer?

Each of these worries could be met, by contrast, in Thailand, a country which Alexander had never even known to exist. Oliver had already filmed there happily, especially for 'Heaven and Earth'. There were excellent film-elephants and an excellent range of professional army-units who were fully accustomed to film service. By early 2003, Jan had fifteen scouts out in the fields, looking for the missing locations. They decided on two: a Botanical garden in Saraburi province, an hour and a half from Bangkok, and a natural plateau in the north at Ubon Ratchathani, overlooking Laos and the Mekong river. The problem at Ubon was that part of the site was a Buddhist holy place and would have to be respected. The problem, to my eye, with the Botanical garden was that it was not a jungle at all. "We're better without it," producer Iain Smith explained: "a real jungle is infested with insects; it keeps on growing; access is awful and if we put elephants in it, they will trample it during the first shot and eat it before the second one". In the Botanical gardens a fine canopy of trees would filter the light and complicate the cavalry, just as the script required. A mock jungle could then be built in a clearing, choosing only plants which elephants would not like to eat.

My other life-long interest is gardening, but by courtesy of Hollywood, I was now attached to a project which put no less than 150 gardeners and $150,000 dollars of ready-grown plants into rock-hard ground during the dry season, so that decorated elephants could thunder through them and charge at me and a hundred others, waiting bare-legged on horses. Maybe the 'light' would be special, but we would be filming during the dry season (as in Morocco) and the director of photography Rodrigo Prieto would be using a bold variety of filters anyway. Was that certain something in a Thai botanical garden the one and only site on earth?

As the film shows, it probably was. For months, I had not even realised that the outdoor locations had had to be hired from their existing owners and then reconstructed. My academic colleagues had visited Morocco and knew that there were pre-built 'film'-forts which tourists could visit: surely we had hired one of them? In fact, the Macedonian theatre was dug out on a field whose owner agreed to hire it for a year in return for rent for his crop. Up to 100,000 tons of earth were then excavated with diggers for the necessary hollow, to be duly returned afterwards. At Vergina, in Macedonia, Philip's real theatre is sited up against the terrace of the royal palace, without any direct view of the sea. The 'film' version, however, lies below a computer-simulated town on the hill above, with a bright blue sea to emphasise the Greek setting. This emphasis proved troublesome. As digging began, the entire theatre had to be shifted slightly to maximise a view of the sea beyond. Just before filming, a heavy autumn storm flooded the theatre interior and left it standing in a foot of water. Drainage-channels had to be dug quickly to clear it out, but here, at least, was another unexpected historical reference. Archaeologists have recently found that the real theatre in Macedonia had drainage channels built into it.

The Gaugamela battlefield was also a first-time film site, but it was brilliantly chosen for its secure distance from any road and its apt background of blue-grey hills. For the horsemen, the scorpions and boulders were an unexpected bonus. By the coast, the other horse-site, Bucephalas's horse-market, was also rather a coup. Oliver wanted the sense of a place in Macedonia to which the nobles and horse-dealers would regularly go in springtime. The field would have to be fresh and green for Bucephalas's taming and his first gallop. Luckily, the nearby sea kept a frequent mist over the fields on this location, ensuring green grass on a flood-plain, even in October. All trucks were kept off the sacred horse-turf, although this ban greatly complicated access and construction: the stones for the market had to be brought in by camel. But the site was a godsend, easily reached from the base at Essaoueira, on the opposite side of the town to the Macedonian theatre. The Bactrian fort was a special challenge. To be dramatic, it had to be steep, but a site on a narrow track to a ski-resort in the Atlas mountains was a choice worthy of Alexander himself. Twice, an avalanche of boulders blocked the approaches at nightfall. As autumn deepened, heavy storms then broke onto the open-air part of it and soaked all the piles of carpets for the wedding party with Roxane's family. Costumes, props and decoration had already had to be carted up from a car-park half a mile away. Now, before midnight, all the carpets and fabrics had to be carted back down the mountains for blow-drying overnight in an industrial laundry in Marrakesh.

Looking through books on Afghanistan, Jan's eye had been caught by the big local mud-brick fortresses with protruding pillars at each of their corner-towers. This image became his springboard for a brilliant castle for Roxane and her family, but as the three lorries and diggers could not reach the site, the entire foundations had to be dug by hand. Construction manager Andy Evans found himself hiring every single Moroccan labourer from the nearest village and praying that only twelve weeks would be enough for assembling a ply-wood and plaster exterior on a frame of metal rods, with mud brick supports specially angled for the occasion. It was a dizzying task which astonished even Oliver: "why have we built Times Square in the Atlas mountains?", he joked with Jan and Andy on seeing the finished results. They had even built walls forty feet high and had moved boulders galore to make a flat surrounding terrace, replacing them with fake rocks where appropriate.

In Morocco, the consequence was a big, helpful spend for the local economy. In spring 2003, an unexpected terrorist attack hit part of Casablanca, causing the production team on 'Troy' to cancel their plans in Morocco and transfer out to Mexico. Intermedia and Oliver preferred to absorb the risk, whatever insurers might think of it. From Mexico, stories then reached our film-army that a freak storm had flattened 'Troy's' Temple of Apollo. The gods were back on our side, and the decision to press on was a turning-point for Morocco's film-industry, otherwise facing a crisis. At Essaoueira, the local district-governor even wanted to keep Oliver's custom-built horse-market standing as a future local attraction.

As one location followed another, I began to realize that Oliver and Jan had caught the Alexander-spirit. The more impossible the site, the more determined Alexander himself had become to conquer it, climbing a vertical rock in Sogdia or an impossible peak near the Himalayas and even joining the island of Tyre to the mainland by an artificial cause-way. Even so, Jan and Oliver remained remarkably harmonious. On our fake jungle site in Thailand, I stood with Jan while Oliver complained in the lunch hour that there were no further trees for the advancing war-elephants to roll over with their trunks. "Don't worry," Jan told him, "there will be a tree there for the afternoon's filming". Sure enough, a truck appeared with a vast mature tree strapped onto it which was then rolled precisely into the elephants' approach-route. How ever, I asked him, did you find a tree in less than an hour? "I knew he was bound to demand one, so I had kept one back in base camp", Jan replied. If you have already designed Pella, Bactria and Babylon together, you do begin to know the ways in which each of you thinks.

Alexander (Colin Farrell) and Ptolemy (Elliot Cowan) are guided by Director Oliver Stone in the 'Hindu Kush' (Morocco's Atlas mountains).

Views through the bedroom in the Babylon Palace.

The Pella Palace has its finishing touches before Philip's wedding.

9. INTERIOR CITIES

Location-hunting, Jan explained to me, is a process of elimination. "You have to try out the alternatives, so that a director is convinced that the eventual choices are the best available. Confidence in the site is crucial. Besides, you never know..." When the hunt goes indoors, it becomes very different: it is not elimination, but evocation.

Out in Morocco, Jan had already conjured up designs for an entry gate into Babylon. He and Oliver were agreed that it should not be Babylon's obvious and most-copied gate, the blue-tiled Ishtar Gate with its animal decoration. It was too much of a cliché. As it happens, it is also the Gate which Saddam Hussein, the self-styled 'new Nebuchadnezzar', had reconstructed with accompanying streets since 1978 on the true site of Babylon in Iraq. Babylon's name meant 'Gate of the Gods' and in Alexander's day, the city had at least seven other big entrance-gates. Oliver's idea was to avoid the corny shot of Babylon shimmering in the distance and instead, to look out from the city to Alexander and then see the scale of the place in shots from Alexander's point of view as he entered one of the other gateways.

Supervising Art Director, Jonathan McKinstry, thus found himself in the heat of a Moroccan summer with the job of building a secondary Gate, to be set in high city-walls. It was as well that Jonathan's previous films included Mission Impossible and Empire of the Sun: the city-walls were to be built to a height of thirty-five feet and the Gate would be even higher, at forty two. The real Babylon had complicated matters by having not one big wall, but two. The film could only afford one, and even so, this wall had to be compressed, as time and money reduced it. The paving slabs for the front of the gateway had to be carved to size by hand and in the strong sun, the blue of the Gate's exterior had to be enlivened by a special perlescent paint-finish. During post-production, the height of both the Gate and the walls were doubled from photographs by the 'visual effects' team in Paris.

For Jan, the Gate was only the threshold of a bigger challenge. In the vast '007' studio in Pinewood, he also took on the responsibility of designing the interior of a big Babylon palace. Here, one and the same set had to accommodate Alexander's triumphal entry, his meeting with the harem and Persian princesses, his final drinking party, his death scenes and, in a side room, the previous death of Hephaestion. Although that death actually happened in history up at Hamadan, it had to be filmed here to save money. Jan then had to draw out whole streets, palaces and temples for the city of Babylon outside the windows, so that computer-graphics could simulate them and insert them into the view.

On joining the film in spring 2002, Jan conjured up mental associations of 'Babylon': what occurred to him first was 'metropolitan', 'luxurious', 'religious', and for some reason a 'land of milk and honey' (which is actually Israel). He also amassed xeroxes of scholars' plans of Babylon, handbooks on ancient Babylonian house styles, streets and the famous stepped temple or 'ziggurat'. This marvel belonged to the huge temple-complex for the god Marduk and was immortalized in the Bible as the 'Tower of Babel'. Research assistants went for him to the New York Public Library and brought xeroxed extracts of any text which came up in English in computerised library-searches. The internet offered the usual Great Flood of information. The results travelled to and fro with Roelfs in files and big suitcases. In them, highlighted passages from tourist-brochures sat side by side with bits of the magisterial Cambridge Ancient History, articles by Alexander expert Brian Bosworth, bits on new views of Babylon by London's specialist Andrew George, extracts on the Bactrian script and language. These cases had a metal-studded look which reminded me of the trunks on the ill-fated Time Life docudrama, but they were much fuller and more relevant.

We live in an age swamped by information; would it not be quicker for film-makers to talk first of all to an expert? Surfing the internet is not true research. But Jan argues that for a film, the process needs to be different. A Production Designer must work out a vision of his own because what he needs is a coherent 'look' which will also feel right to the audience. He is not engaged in objective documentary history, but he is engaged in carrying an audience subjectively with him, and audiences bring their own hazy mental images to great names like Babylon, Greece or Alexandria. Sometimes these images have developed from paintings by Orientalist or Neo-classical artists in the nineteenth century. No film wants to show the same old sets, but if a film goes way out into new (often disputed) territory, the audience will lose their 'feel' of the historic scene. The true 'look' of the past can shock, whereas an action-film cannot afford to look too 'wrong' and bemuse its viewers.

Information fed Roelfs's visions, and then he started to draw. Babylon must be vast, but it must also have the feel of an old city in Alexander's times. There are plenty of modern plans of Babylon, especially the famous models in the Berlin museum. However, the models represent Babylon at one of its earlier high points, at least 250 years before Alexander. During the early sixth century BC, the Babylonian King Nebuchadnezzar rebuilt the city entirely after its destruction by a previous Assyrian conqueror. Even then, there is much uncertainty: the city was first studied by German archaeologists in the 1890's, but the excavations found heavily-ruined remains whose interpretation is still highly disputed.

Rightly, Jan aimed for touches of Persian detail: the overall look was freer, like nineteenth century Orientalism. For the tone of the main palace-interiors, Jan was drawn to a shade of deep blue as the walls' main colour. Oliver, preferring red and gold, was at first unconvinced: would it "look like a swimming pool?" But we know that Babylon's big Ishtar gate was tiled in blue: blue could be repeated in blocks on some of the exterior facades for the long shots of the city: blue would give a rich impression of the ageing which Alexander needed to encounter. To emphasise the Persian era, Jan looked across to the palaces at Susa and Persepolis whose kings had occupied Babylon for some two hundred years. So, the Babylon interior would have tall fluted columns, back-to-back bulls on their capitals and coloured hangings from the pillars up by the coffered roof. The set was to be extremely high, but by a master-stroke Jan varied the levels up and down the stairways so that the cameras following Alexander would sometimes pick up the tops of his 'Persian' architecture in a room below. On the stairways, as he gained confidence, he put moulded figures of courtiers in procession, just as on the famous stairways at Persepolis and the Assyrian palaces, their model. The blue plaster-walls were patterned with imitations of the ancient Babylonian wedge-shaped, or cuneiform, script, another fine historical reference.

The Babylon set also had to have light and city views on all sides, looking out with horizontal vistas onto the simulated city. In the doorways, Jan decided on pierced wooden screens, to be made by hand in Morocco. Only Hephaestion's fatal bed-room had to strike a chill, gloomy note. Here the colour was made sombre and the walls were given a simpler, Egyptian-style look. Alexander, by contrast, died in the Persians' former royal bedroom, beneath a hanging symbol of the Persian god Ahura Mazda, as if it had been left behind by King Darius's court. After experiments with a sandstone colouring, its pillars, too, were painted a black shade to suggest granite. As there were several palaces anyway in Nebuchadnezzar's rebuilt Babylon, none of whose interior is at all well attested, another pastiche at Pinewood was not a transgression. In his last days, we hear of Alexander crossing over the Euphrates to 'the palace', but we do not know which one: we do, however, hear of him spending time by a 'swimming pool', a support for Jan's choice of 'Babylon blue'. So impressive was the palace-set that pieces of it were eventually donated to the British Museum for their store-room and for display in their forthcoming exhibition on the Persian era and its legacy.

The city outside was as big a challenge for its artists: it would be disastrous to have 'great sets, awful scenery'. Here, Jan worked with concept-artist Adam Brockbank, whose business was to design the city in perspective, so that 'visual effects' could insert it into the palace-views and the army's scenes of welcome. Film visions of Babylon have tended, famously, towards the totalitarian style of modern fascist dictatorships or the slabs of a futuristic American city. Jan wanted a clear, 'metropolitan' look along the river Euphrates, and so he alternated blue and brown facades and kept the buildings' windows small. There are two celebrated problems in Babylon's city-plan, the 'Tower of Babel' and the 'Hanging Gardens'. The 'Tower' was a sort of pyramid (called 'Etumananki') in the huge temple precinct, which also contained the enormous 'Esagila' shrine (the 'Temple of the Heights'). The Alexander-historians do state clearly that this shrine had been damaged badly by a previous Persian King (Xerxes, they said) and that Alexander ordered it to be rebuilt. In his absence, the priests did nothing, preferring (it was said) to keep the income of the site for themselves. Jan drew a damaged ziggurat (in my view, correctly) to be visible on the army's march-past. As the real one is calculated to have had 36 million bricks, the construction team was thankful that it was to be computer-simulated.

The 'Hanging Gardens' have also become controversial. The Oxford expert, Stephanie Dalley, has recently argued that they were never actually in Babylon, but rather in Nineveh. She explained her research to Jan, who was opposed to palm-trees in Babylon itself, as he personally hates them and finds them a cliché in California. In fact, Babylon's palms were very famous, and so the 'visual effects' discreetly soften the architecture with green 'trees' at a distance. The elusive 'Hanging Gardens' were not shown in detail but were symbolised indoors by long, drooping stems of fake green asparagus-fern which from the upper pillars inside the Palace. They were a deliberate example of playing metaphorically on an audience's expectations. The real Hanging Gardens were outdoor terraced gardens with trees, but this indoor 'hanging greenery' softened the palace interior and added a 'feel' with which viewers could identify. It looked stunning, and like all great sets, it stimulated the actors and the way they played the scenes.

Whereas Babylon was extremely complex, the buildings of Macedon's Pella were governed by simple conventions. In the 1990's Greek archaeologists located the probable site of the 'Pella palace' on a hill at the Macedonian site. They have revealed nothing, as yet, of its appearance, so Jan developed a well-known Greek architecture of Doric colonnades with suitable roof-tiling, to fill in what archaeology has yet to uncover. The challenge here was for concept-artist Simon Thorpe. The frieze on the Pella gymnasium was the least of his problems. Jan showed him scenes of men boxing and wrestling on Greek painted pottery and within an hour, Simon had drawn out the athletic figures for the building's white background. The challenge, rather, was the Cave scene, complete with rats, which Oliver had imagined for Philip and the young Alexander beneath the Pella palace. Naturally, there is no historical evidence of such caves or their mythical paintings, but the scene is such a vivid way of introducing Alexander as to. Medea, Jason and Oedipus...: their stories connect deliberately to strong, vindictive women, like Alexander's own mother, and the Titans are grimly down there too, or still inside us all. Simon began by drawing out paintings to be attached to a mock rock-face: Oliver felt they were "too classical... too English... too restrained". His aim was to show very old 'Dark Age' graffiti, so Simon was urged by Oliver to look to Tibetan rock-art or to the prehistoric cave paintings in France's Lascaux. So, his style changed to one of scratchy white lines which would undulate on the rock face itself. Half-lit by Val Kilmer's torch, they would then seem to flicker a simple horror "as if seen through a boy's eyes", as Oliver was urging.

Following Oliver's lead, Simon found hints for Medea's face in Tibetan art, while the famous picture of a pregnant mammoth in the Lascaux caves solved his problem of showing father Cronos devouring his children. The children would be shown inside him, like the 'mini-mammoths' who are shown inside their Lascaux mother. For five hard weeks, Simon worked at drawing his computer-based images onto rough plaster. The scale was extremely difficult, as the images had to be seen through a boy's eyes, looking nervously up from ground level. The 'movie show' on the walls was to be 58 feet long, and the Achilles panel alone had to be 16 feet high to be in scale for the camera. Horses seen at Lascaux inspired the horses which were shown dragging Hector's body behind Achilles' chariot. This semi-mythical scene, as Oliver artfully intended, was then repeated in Olympias' bedroom above ground, this time in a classical, more 'modern' Greek style. Just before filming, Oliver insisted here that Simon should remove another charioteer and should concentrate on Achilles, the key figure for Alexander. "There's no such thing as a wild Englishman", Oliver had told him on first seeing the tunnel: was Oedipus's myth being shown with sufficient sex and violence? But in Simon, as he soon realised, his scene found a wild master. The 'tunnel' had to be cut away on one side so that the camera could follow Philip as he lit up the scenes of Cronos by his torch, but somehow Simon kept the scale and even, at the last minute, added an extra Titan to match Val Kilmer's route.

For Jan, the next challenge to be filmed was the Indian palace, scene of the dreadful murder of Cleitus. In India, there is no archaeology of the period on which to build. Visiting Greeks describe towns with wooden walls and towers, but they give no clues about a palace's interior. Jan decided to use wood as a contrast to Babylon's solid pillars, and then to add his own eclectic mix of Indian elements, Mogul, filmic or loosely based on patterns from the sixth to tenth centuries AD. A pool with lotus-leaves enhanced the 'feel': however, Oliver queried it on the afternoon before filming started, and to convince him, Jan had it filled in. It was then reinstated when Oliver saw for himself how much it contributed. Of all the indoor sets, India was the one where Jan could have most fun, with candles, niches, awnings and imaginary architecture.

To my eye, however, Alexandria and its library were the most impressive set of all. Film-goers naturally think of Egypt as old and honey-coloured in a setting of sand and sandstone. But Jan wanted to show a newly-built Greek city of the future, forty years after Alexander's death. Remarkably, we have no ancient evidence for the appearance of this city's great library, but Jan envisaged it in grey, white and black, to suggest granite, not sandstone, pillars. In the last ten years, underwater archaeology has taught us much more about the submerged areas of the Ptolemies' Alexandria and a re-use of the old Egyptian dark black columns has emerged as important. Jan had hit it right, and he and Senior Art Director Kevin Phipps enjoyed developing a new style of Greco-Egyptian pillar-capitals for the columns in Ptolemy's personal study. The shape of the room, however, had to change. Initially, the plan was to build an even bigger set across two linked studios at Shepperton to allow a square-shaped study. The costing reduced it to one studio, and so Jan chose a circular design, something which would have been rather avant garde in Ptolemy's day. Out of a budget-cut, something even better emerged.

Leading off the study, Jan had imagined a passage-wall covered with documents, the starting-point for his thinking about the entire library: "a theatre of documents", which Oliver and others at first could not envisage. With Kevin, Jan developed an artful arrangement of the scrolls in angled niches, not in normal pigeon-holes: 'visual effects' would then fill in the vast library beyond and the study roof which had been left bare for studio lighting. Kevin set to work, imitating a fragmentary ancient floor-mosaic which had recently been unearthed in Alexandria during the construction of the city's new Unesco-sponsored Library. On the wall, the 'mosaics' of hunting include copies of two other ancient mosaics found at Pella: the battle-scenes showing Colin (Alexander) are Jan and Kevin's neat touch. Again, visual effects would insert the background view of Alexandria, stretching down to the harbour and its famous wonder, its Lighthouse. But the balcony on which Ptolemy (Anthony Hopkins) first speaks to us was shaped by Oliver himself. He had visited Athens to talk with the composer of the film's music, Vangelis Papathanassiou, and he returned with a clear impression of the famous composer's own Greek balcony. So he agreed something similar with Jan: potted plants of Egyptian papyrus combined with an echo of modern Athens to make up Alexandria.

Back on the 007 stage at Pinewood, construction manager Andy Evans was thankful to hear that the part of the Persian Queen Mother had been removed from the script; he was spared one more bedroom on the Babylon palace-set. Now 48, Andy had begun his film-career as a carpenter in Star Wars, working on the Millennium Falcon spaceship: he came to Alexander from such films as 'Shakespeare in Love' and 'Around the World in 80 days'. He now had to go 'around the ancient world' in even less, helped by construction-teams who fluctuated between 250 and 500 members. Andy gave me a list of the basic materials which the indoor sets on the '007' stage had used up. They include '10 miles of tube', '4 miles of timber, 6" by 2"', '750 rolls of canvas' and an amazing '300 tonnes of plaster'. The list does not include Alexandria's needs, equally vast at Shepperton. Running a budget of $10 million, Andy was thankful for his trade-contacts, the unsurpassed skills of British plasterers and set-painters and the infectious determination which Jan and his designers generated. Until September, he had even been assuming that some of the jungle scenes would be filmed in Morocco, so that the return to Pinewood would begin three weeks later. He was also assuming that Alexandria in Shepperton would be filmed first. The 'jungle' transferred to Thailand and Hopkins's schedule meant that Shepperton had to wait until after Christmas. So Babylon came forwards, unfinished. Andy measures his life not by years but by the films on which he is working. The race against time for Alexander is not a phase he will forget.

For Jan, the sets were windows onto irresistible new worlds. "I know what they expected…", he told me later on the Babylon set, "a liberal Dutchman, brought up in Holland, with open-plan bedrooms and a glass bathroom", but the scale and the shapes of the wonders of the ancient world had grown to fascinate him. And what next? "I'd most of all like to design another ancient movie: Carthage maybe, or ancient Athens". Off his pencilled scraps of paper, the lost cities of Babylon and Alexandria had taken memorable shape. As I reflected on it all with the supervising Art Director, Jonathan McKinstry, he smiled at the domestic building-plans at his home in Surrey. "Alexander conquered Babylon, it is true," he told me, "but we are the ones who built it, and we built it quicker than two new bathrooms in my house".

Oliver Stone and Rodrigo Prieto inspect the view of Babylon on a camera-monitor in English midwinter.

The gorgeous harem of ladies in the Babylon Palace.

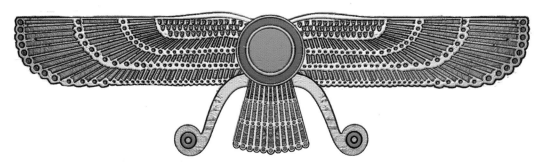

A pre-production drawing of the Persian-style winged disc, accompaniment of the god Ahura Mazda, in the Babylon Palace.

Opposite page: Pre-production drawing for Queen Eurydice's carriage in Macedonia.

10. Time Travelling

As the sets and locations were built up, they all had to be furnished. There were to be bedrooms, tents, halls and a harem. There would also be battlefields with war-chariots, elephants and thundering cavalry-horses. The ancient histories of Alexander tell us remarkably little about the decorative aspects of his life. In his later years, they remark, with a hint of disapproval, that Alexander had a golden throne and his companions would dine on couches whose legs were made of silver. There is only one glimpse of an interior, the vast reception-tent in which Alexander celebrated the weddings of himself and his officers to Iranian brides at Susa in 324 BC. It survives in the words of Alexander's own Master of Ceremonies who describes an amazing 'tent-city' with ninety-two separate rooms, one for each bridal couple. There were pillars thirty feet high plated with gold, silver and jewels, there were lavish textiles and gold and silver curtain-rods for curtains embroidered with gold and the figures of animals. It was fortunate for the production's budget that Oliver's Script Draft 4 had had to bring forward these Iranian weddings and merge them all with Roxane's in Bactria, thereby cutting out a separate scene at Susa.

As Production Designer, Jan was responsible for the 'look' of every detail, but by May 2003 he had assembled a skilled Set team. The main Set Decorator was to be Jim Erickson, a quietly-spoken veteran of 54 years, widely admired for his work on 'The Last of the Mohicans' and 'Seven Years in Tibet'. His Associate, David Balfour, brought a Scottish realism and ingenuity as Head of Props with teams ranging from Pinewood across to Bangkok. In every corner of the production, ingenious craftsmen and designers descended on the ancient world, giving days of thought to authentic shields, scrolls or the details of bowls and drinking-cups. An entire armoury was set up at Pinewood under the direction of the Head Armourer, Richard Hooper.

The arrival of this team gave historians, too, a new role. In late May, the heads of departments asked if they could visit Oxford for meetings with experts and archaeologists from the University. Academic life is not usually organised by 'movement orders', but the patient Katie Gabriel, co-ordinator at Pinewood, coped with the changing dates and timings of the personnel. The 'Oxford Meeting' was then expanded to include Jan and Oliver. May is a frantic time in University life and with hindsight, I realise how I had underestimated the scope of the film-makers' plans and their willingness to draw on expert advice. From the younger post-doctoral generation, Fiona Rose gave clear guidelines on how best to stage the sacrifice of a bull and whether a wrestling-match should be naked on the sand in Pella's gymnasium. Lindsay Allen suggested sources for East Iranian dances, necessarily of a later date, and answered questions on Persian textiles and possible shapes for Alexander's Babylon bed. Judith MacKenzie addressed the changing face of Alexandria, but she verified, too, the validity of the yellow-red finger-ring, acquired by Hephaestion in Egypt and given to Alexander: just such a coloured stone, she pointed out, is now mentioned in a newly-discovered papyrus text of poems by the early Alexandrian Greek poet, Poseidippus. Stephanie Dalley, Oxford's expert in Babylonian studies, saw it as her role at least to "present to the film-makers what the present state of knowledge is". She rightly insisted on the dust and dirt of Babylon's streets and the presence of people busied with pumping and carrying water. She also gave Jan a beautifully-drawn sketch of Babylon's city-centre, not expecting it to do much to change his mind. "Production Designers have big egos", Jan reminded me afterwards, but he listened gratefully to Stephanie's theories on the non-existence of Babylon's 'Hanging Gardens'. In February, at the British Museum, I had also met Lloyd Llewellyn-Jones, a specialist in Greek and Persian costumes. Available in Oxford, he became the Production team's most constant visitor, going over to Pinewood more than thirty times.

I had no idea, either, how much would have to be designed and made afresh. There have been no big Greek epics of this period and as nothing much could be hired, the 'Alexander' team made four-fifths of the objects required. "We felt as if we were time-travellers", David Balfour later recalled to me: one of their first travels backwards in time was from Pinewood studio to the seventeenth-century Panelled Room at New College, Oxford. Here, round the big dining room table, they put questions to Oxford specialists whose answers were recorded on tape. Should Alexander's bed be decorated with an eagle (Oliver wanted an eagle to pick up on his link between Alexander and Prometheus, the mythical eagle's victim)? How did ancient Greeks bathe? How high were their couches? The set team had observed important differences in the levels at which the film's various peoples sat or reclined. From vase-paintings, it appeared that Greeks dined reclining on rather high couches, certainly when compared with the furniture later used in India. To focus the Pinewood team's ideas, I brought some of the recent books on archaeological finds in their areas; Andronicos's great Macedonian discoveries at Vergina, Stella Miller's account of a painted Macedonian tomb which has the best (later) representations of Macedonian armour, the study of Persepolis's column-capitals and coloured hangings by Shahpur Shahbazi, the Iranian Director of Persepolis in the 1970's under the Shah's rule. These sites and their sources became starting-points for the Pinewood team's own rapid researches.

There was also the difficult question of music. Oliver was wondering if the film might be set to a replay of ancient Greek music: what do we know about it and can we research it? One of the great experts on the subject had kindly agreed to attend, but he was rightly unable to give any guidance about the correct sort of music at particular points in the story. Even the Greeks' instruments are hard to reconstruct with certainty. What would have been played, Oliver asked, at a fourth-century wedding to Roxane in Bactria? We simply do not know. "Well, I'm staging another wedding, this time in fourth century Macedonia:

Pre-production image of the interior of Alexander's campaign tent at Gaugamela.

Achilles shown dragging the dead Hector behind his chariot among skeletons on the walls of the Pella caves.

Parmenion (John Kavanagh) disputes with Alexander (Colin Farrell) about his plans in the Bactrian council chamber.

Pre-production drawing for the bedcover of Roxane, Alexander's bride.

what sort of music should we play there?" Correctly, the expert view was that we have no idea. Oliver was becoming impatient: "Professor, I'm offering you a chance to impose your view of ancient music on millions of people for the next ten years, and are you trying to tell me that you do not even know what it was? What is this book of yours on the subject: is it a how-to-do-it manual, or is there some secret here that you're hiding, like the recipe for Coca Cola?" There is no hidden recipe, and as a result the music for the film was handed over to the famous Greek composer, Vangelis Papathanassiou, for modern elaboration in Athens.

I had never imagined that this 'set' team would make such constant reference back to the Oxford specialists during the next twelve weeks or that particular objects would be researched and designed with such a remarkable concern for historical origins. As the evening finished, Oliver was keen that the younger Oxford specialists, particularly, should have a chance to make their views known on set: it would be fun and helpful, he decided, and so during the November schedule in England both Fiona and Lindsay would find themselves being chauffeured from Oxford to Pinewood to comment on action on the Pella and Babylon stages. As we walked back through the New College gardens in the twilight, Oliver noticed the impressive stairway up its central feature, an ornamental Garden Mound. "Let's run up it", he suggested, "and sacrifice a goat at the top". Dionysus was enjoying himself, but there was no goat available and no Fiona to give instructions. In only three months time, would there be any more sign of the interior decorations which we had discussed?

Their co-ordination owes much to Jim Erickson, although ancient history had never been his field of study. Jim had grown up in Badger, Minnesota, a "Lutheran Christian community of some 200 souls", many of whom are of Norwegian origin. He had trained in drama, but in 2001 he had enjoyed Homer's Odyssey in translation. He now found himself designing sets about four centuries later than Homer's date. Jim modestly defines his aim as to see "that my work should not be noticed". His decoration has to reinforce the mood and look of a film, but never monopolise it. That aim involved him in patient study in London's British and Victoria and Albert Museums, in Oxford's Ashmolean and in scores of related source-books. The 'decoration' budget was set at some $5 million and Jim and David Balfour were clear that the forthcoming film on Troy must not distort their sense of period. 'Troy's' 'events' were set in an era so far from Alexander's own.

Jim decided on a progression of splendour. In antiquity, Macedon was rich in silver, as the contents of Philip's tomb confirm, but also, as archaeology continues to prove, in a use of gold which was lavish by ancient Greek standards. However, Jim preferred to keep the Macedonian style quite simple, silver rather than gold, and then to build up to golden luxury in the Babylonian bedrooms. Early on in the film, we meet one of his masterpieces, the hangings round Olympias's bed while she sings her lullaby to the young Alexander, 'mosquito-nets' as Jim saw them. On the walls behind, the paintings give the impression of mosaics with scenes of the Persian War and other appropriate Greek myths. For the bed-hangings, Jim bought a specially-woven pattern of grapes and snakes, themes which picked up Olympias's 'Dionysiac' behaviour. He found the right material in a display-roll at a trade fair in England's Cotswolds: it was woven in Iran, but rising to the occasion, its suppliers then came up with another 300 metres at short notice. Silver snakes emphasised Olympias's living basketful of them, and as the film progressed, Jim artfully matched the changing emotions by changing the set decoration too. Olympias ended, he felt, in increasing paranoia and finally in grief at Alexander's death. So, he envisaged her retreating into a 'cage' of tapestry, ending among a fringe of black material, made in Morocco for keeping flies off the horses and camels. It surrounded her 'like black prison bars', with red tassels, a far cry from the white drapes of her earlier scenes.

In her room, Olympias, he assumed, might work at a loom, like Homer's Penelope in the Odyssey. Around her, every single bowl, cup or plate had to be manufactured specially, to convey the general effect which Jim now had clearly in his head. Sometimes, he asked for the drawings to be exact historical copies. For the Macedonian drinking cups, Jim chose replicas of the silver cups which had been found recently in the royal Vergina tomb. They were then made quickly in Moroccan metal workshops. For Roxane's castle, he and the team sketched out heavy silver vessels with chased figures of lions attacking deer and 'palmette' patterns on their undersides. These classic Iranian motifs were copied from museum-items, while David Balfour exploited reference-books of the Greek pottery in Russia's Hermitage Museum for suitable shapes and accompanying vase-paintings. Above all, in Alexander's Babylon bedroom, Jim commissioned two big imitations of a remarkable bronze mixing-bowl for wine, which had been discovered quite recently at Derveni on Macedon's borders. This huge, brassy object dates to the era of King Philip and is decorated with orgiastic scenes of Dionysus and his Maenads, possibly alluding to Euripides's great drama, The Bacchae. This vase has a showy splendour which is suggestive of the drinking-parties, too, in Philip's Macedonian society. Jim's two copies were cast in styrofoam and were coloured gold, to suggest the exceptional luxury in Alexander's last years. They were a clever allusion to Alexander's new riches and his capacity for Dionysiac excess.

The colour-range of the Babylonian set struck Jim as a 'peacock's feather' with blue and gold predominating. For the death scene, Oliver had rightly forbidden a four-poster bed, but the final choice, with lions' heads and scenes of battles and hunting, could only be made in time in Bangkok. No less than seventy embroidered panels also had to be commissioned as hangings between the palace pillars, while Jan's dislike of palm-trees meant that the palace-hall needed a different floral look. For colour, Jim opted for cymbidium-orchids, confessing that Babylonian plant-hunters had "perhaps made unacknowledged visits to the Far East". For the harem scene, last-minute attention was caught by a superb sculpted panel, published in the London newspapers as the British Museum's latest acquisition. It showed a full-breasted lady, probably a goddess, with bird-like feet and an accompanying owl. The Museum had named her 'Lady of the Night', recognising her as a very rare Old Babylonian carving from 1800 BC. Earlier scholars had even suggested that she might have been an emblem on a Babylonian brothel. This new arrival was too good to miss: the visual effects team were allowed by the Museum to photograph their 'night-lady' and insert her as a presiding figure in Oliver's harem. Her replica was then given to him by the set-crew as a film-memento.

This backbone of 'historical' imitation was supported by a careful buying of carpets, low tables, 'Oriental' objects and appropriate curiosities. On the chairs among Persian scenery, carved pine-cones and pomegranates picked up elements attested in Iranian sculpture and military equipment. On the floors of Babylon, several of the carpets recalled patterns on the rare surviving carpets which have been found in the frozen tombs of Pazyryk, up in Scythia, dating to the fifth century BC. On the floor of Colin's command-tent in Bactria, the carpet-style was made more 'tribal': it was bought in batches in Morocco's warehouses. Wherever wall-paintings were needed, artists painted scenes of hunting, battle or mythology in the Macedonian rooms after studying mosaics from Pella or vase-paintings from fifth or fourth century Greece. On the set, the 'illusion of reality' was devised by consulting reality, but not by being governed by it.

The furnishing of Ptolemy's Alexandrian study was a special pleasure for Jim. Consulting with Judith MacKenzie, he decided that old Ptolemy would have amassed a collection of curiosities befitting a former pupil of the philosopher and natural historian, Aristotle. Desks were a historical problem, but out in Marrakesh he found a nineteenth-century Venetian table with a marble top which would fit neatly with Kevin Phipps' floor-mosaic. In a London Chelsea antiques shop, he then found a hippopotamus-skull for hire, suggestive of Egypt's natural history. In every niche of Jan's 'document wall', scribes busily copied labels and bits of Greek text for Judith's suggested list of the Greek literary masterpieces which would have existed, still, in Ptolemy's Library. The team became carried away with the details, and visiting the set in December, I felt a pang of regret at all the Greek texts which had been lost to us since antiquity. They were lovingly labelled here and imitated for a long camera-shot which could never do justice to all this film-scholarship.

One of the biggest problems was the tenting. For Jim's Indian palace, in which Gary Stretch was to be murdered, Jim began by commissioning a great canopy of heavy fabric. In London's Portobello Antiques Market, he found samples of a superb antique textile embroidered with the stars and moon. He bought it on sight, commissioned copies twenty five meters square, but then found that as a roofing it was too thick and excluded too much light. Jan wanted an outdoor 'feel' to the fatal dinner-party and proposed a plain, thin canopy of orange silk instead. It was less exotic, but more effective and even Jim felt the change was an improvement.

The campaign tents of Alexander and the Persian Kings were much more difficult. The Persian tent could be developed with later Ottoman-style emboidery, but Alexander's tent would have to be imagined without any evidence, and it would also have to survive sand-storms, wind and a move all the way from Morocco to Thailand. Jim was a regular visitor to the trade-fairs at Kempton Park Racecourse outside London where he suddenly spotted a roll of heavy linen, hand-woven in Romania, 'by gypsies', he was told. As cotton was not yet used by Macedonians, the fabric would be particularly appropriate: the problem was that he needed no less than 2500 meters of it. Back in Romania, the suppliers worked overtime to meet this order of a lifetime. Meanwhile, Jim set about realising his mind's eye view of the interior. On the tent's fabric he fixed appliqué leather panels depicting the mythical labours of Heracles, ancestor of the Macedonian kings. On a table, Alexander would then move, not twigs and bottle-caps, but big clay-based models of cavalrymen and infantrymen, finished with resin to resemble ivory. Oliver and Colin were aware that the film's action-scenes had laid too little emphasis on Alexander's planning and clever practicality. By giving him the world's first 'model soldiers' – why not? - Jim and David could hint at Alexander's advance strategy and forethought. So, too, on his command-desk, Oliver was keen that there should be practical plans and models, hoists, water-systems and lists of facts and figures. Here, too, a subtle 'set-dressing' emphasised what the drama could only hint at in its script.

From the start, the team had taken wholeheartedly to the challenge. For them all, the fourth century BC was wholly new ground, with the added dimension of Persian, Indian and Bactrian cultures. But the objects in books and museums were so appealing, and at the end of a four-month marathon, David Balfour told me he had only one regret: "Alexander should have lived on, and done even more, so that we could all go on and on". On most other films, the set-directors start to compromise and give in to the restrictions of the schedule.

From all this inventive imitation, questions kept flying back to the Oxford team. Fiona specified Macedonian details and how to conduct an animal sacrifice correctly, using a knife, a basket of barley and water: the set-team then arranged a dummy dead bull, oozing plastic entrails. For Babylon, Lindsay set out details of the big Persian emblem which would hover evocatively over Alexander's final bed: it was run up in Pakistan. All the while questions kept pouring into me. How did the troops light a fire? Should dead Persians show body hair? What spices should the eunuch Bagoas scatter on the dying Alexander (they were duly sourced in London and put in an Egyptian-style bag)? In Jim's and David's vision, there was an exceptional concern for these touches of realism. At times, they bring audiences up with a surprise. To a modern eye, the bronze Greek statues may look too shiny, but Alexander's, unlike ours, were not green antiques. The painted images of the gods in Philip's fatal theatre-procession at Aigai began, certainly, by looking too bright, too 'wrong' for a modern eye. But the furnishings were usually based on a springboard of historical study. Every single tool had to be made for the craftsmen who were to be filmed following Alexander's army. However, the metal 'spike' which kills one of Alexander's wounded men was a non-negotiable element of the Director's wide reading.

Equally, academic input could be catastrophic too. It was for me to send copies of the Greek maps, showing Aristotle's distorted view of the world and then Ptolemy's slightly bigger view of it on his study-wall c.285 BC, fifty years after Alexander's march. The clearest images were in an old nineteenth-century volume on ancient geography in New College library. I sent copies of them to the set-painters, forgetting that the place-names were all given in Latin, a language which Ptolemy and his Alexandrians did not yet know. On set, I was then mortified to see Anthony Hopkins advancing to a well-shaped wall map on which the names of 'Aegyptus' and the 'Mediterraneum' were entered in anachronistic Latin. It was my fault, but typically, Oliver ordered the map to be re-labelled and then re-shot for insertion by visual effects into the film background.

Alexander (Colin Farrell) among his new Bactrian friends at his wedding to Roxane.

Tent interior sc.50

ab019

The changed appearance of Alexander's tent, now out in Bactria.

Alexander (Colin Farrell) on King Darius's former throne with the Shield of Achilles behind.

There remained the challenge of the armoury and the dressings of the animals for war. Richard Hooper had already located the expert summaries by Polish scholar Nick Sekunda and the English war-historian, Peter Connolly. On their theories and surviving art-works, the armoury of the Macedonian soldiers was developed, with further advice from Connolly on the shape of the infantry-lances, or sarissas, and the likeliest angle for a cavalryman's charge with a spear and no stirrups. Teams of armourers then ran off model shields in polyurethane, marked with the Macedonian star-emblem which is attested in archaeology. Metal helmets, inevitably, were too expensive, but the polyurethane copies were all based on historical prototypes. There was one special exception: the celebrated 'Shield of Achilles' which Alexander carried with him after taking it from the city of Troy. Like the heroic Alexander, a wounded Colin would be carried on it to safety from his Indian attackers. Richard Hooper gave this briefly-seen object particular care. He consulted a reconstruction of it in the Ashmolean museum in Oxford, which is based on Homer's exquisite description in his epic poem, the Iliad Book Eighteen. He researched evidence on the internet and then opted for an older reconstruction, proposed in the 1930's. The drawing was assigned to Finlay Cowan, whose previous work included art-work for the pop group Pink Floyd. Brilliantly, he composed the concentric pattern of pictures, based on Homeric verses, and added, as a post-Homeric touch, a central Gorgon's head. The background was silvered with a gilded surface and acetoned in places so that 'gold' would show through. The wide span was then fixed by an aluminium central disc. It is a high point of imaginative reconstruction, one more proof of how artists with a non-classical training could quickly run off a classicising imitation. My ideas of the classics' appeal were transformed by the outside craftsmen who rose to these challenges.

Last but not least, there were details for the animals. At Gaugamela the Persian king had fiercely scythed chariots, and Jonathan McKinstry had seen drawings of them fitted with a central bar between their horses and a yoke on the horses' shoulders. In Morocco, the horses would be smaller, able to take only a maximum of 75 kilos. At the back of the chariot therefore, the axle and its mountings had to be moved forwards so as to redistribute weight on the horse teams. Assistant Horsemaster Pedro Perero was most unwilling to risk Jonathan's ancient system, but he did then remember seeing a type of neck yoke which worked safely, and so the chariot-horses, with their coats of gilded plates, were able to pull freely through the sand. Six chariots were commissioned for permanent use, with two as spares, and although they had to be heavier than the real Persian originals, they came through their ordeal without too much damage. They were then passed on to the film-carriage farm of Steve Dent; they live on in England at Beaconsfield near Pinewood.

The main problem in dressing the cavalry horses was to devise a workable type of horse blanket. If the blankets slipped or tore, the cavalry-charges would be chaotic: assistant Armourer, Tracy Miller, opted for waxed, shaven hides of 'upholstery cows' which she bought from specialist upholsterers Halls by London Bridge. They proved very smooth and comfortable for our bare legs, with the advantage of hiding the small Moroccan saddles to whose girths they were pinned. For the Persian cavalry, by contrast, burgundy-coloured blankets were made up from felt and chenille, while for Colin's distinct presence, there was to be a simulated leopard skin on black Bucephalas' back. Tracy based this idea on Angus McBride's coloured illustration of Alexander in battle in one of the English 'Osprey' books: this picture, in turn, is based on archaeological traces of such animal skins on the backs of painted Macedonian cavalry-horses. As a real leopard skin would be too small and unavailable, Tracy shaved the hair off a cow-skin, painted it tawny brown and applied leopard-sized black dots all over it. For Colin alone, ten reserve 'leopard blankets' were needed to stand the strain. By Thailand only two remained intact.

The star attractions, of course, were the Thai elephants. No image of elephants in Alexander's time shows any elaborate dress or howdah on them: one scholar has even suggested that the howdah may be a later Greek invention. For a film, however, the war-elephants would have to be made more vivid. The answer was to look ahead to the bright costumes which were used in later Indian elephant-battles, including those of the Mogul emperors in the seventeenth century.

The task of 'elephant-dressing' was ascribed to Stuart Rose and his team, and the problems were formidable. Each elephant is of a different size and shape and when it drinks or eats, it may add up to two feet temporarily onto its girth. Twenty sets of golden-plated armour were designed with pink, orange and green decorations, and on seven elephants, howdahs were commissioned too. Stuart battled to find a workable weight of howdah which would stay firm and yet contain warriors inside it. He had to experiment, and he found that foam rubber padding was needed to hold the equipment steady. The 'saddle' cloths also had to be thick enough to take a volley of dummy arrows. The elephants' foreheads must be decorated too, but it would be left to their owner Sompast Meerpan at his 'Elephant Palace' in Thailand, to fit tusk-extensions onto those elephants whose natural tusks were too short or broken.

From December onwards, Stuart worked to fit his exotic armoury onto each beast in the line. Each steel-framed howdah had to be painted and its supports had to be toned down to green, orange and ochre. Above all, the elephants had to accept them. For a day, all the body-equipment was laid out on the ground in front of them so that they could feel it over with their trunks and become familiar with it at leisure. At this rehearsal, the elephants, Stuart saw, were 'fantastically placid'. Next, it was their full dress rehearsal, but one of them was equipped with ankle-straps which had not been presented to it on the day before. Stuart watched in amazement as the animal lowered its trunk, unbuckled the decorated strap from its foot and brought it up to have a good look at it. It was an awesome reminder of these beasts' intelligence. It then laid the strap on the ground and accepted it back onto its foot. There could be no more touching tribute to the 'set dressing' of the film.

Opposite page: Robin Lane Fox demonstrates a sarissa position to the unpersuaded Captain Dale Dye.

11. Warriors Incorporated

Alexander's life was one of fighting and battles, but which battles should the film choose to show? Early versions of the script focussed only on the battle of Chaeronea, the famous battle in 338BC in which Philip defeated the armies of the Athenians and other opposing states in Greece. Chaeronea was a turning point in Greek history and in the history of political freedom, "fatal to liberty" as the poet John Milton called it, and its battlefield, with a burial mound for the dead, is still preserved and honoured in central Greece. Alexander fought here as a young prince, only 18 years old, and was said by our only account of the action to have led the cavalry down the wing in a decisive charge. The battle would have the advantage of showing Philip and Alexander together and would present the essential elements of the army, Philip's creation. But it was not one of Alexander's own triumphs and it was not in an exotic location.

As soon as Oliver took over the final writing of the script, the military scenes became much more ambitious. Alexander's greatest victory in Asia, the battle of Gaugamela, became the first great action scene of the film. In India, a forest battle against elephants would then symbolise the experiences of the army against these terrifying beasts, the increasing reluctance of his troops and the wounding of Alexander himself and his horse. These choices imposed far greater challenges on the experts in clothing and armoury. At Gaugamela, Alexander had fought against a huge army from the central and eastern districts of the Persian King's empire, including Bactrians from what is now Afghanistan, Royal 'Immortal' guards and range of weaponry and costume which were much more spectacular than the ranks of metal-armoured Greeks which Philip had faced in Greece at Chaeronea. In the Indian battle, war-elephants would confront horses and cavalry, something which no film-maker had ever attempted before. Unlike the Greeks, the Indian army was equipped with longbows and yet another style of dress. Above all, these battles were not a rifle-and-artillery sort of shoot-out in which the generals remained safely behind the lines, while their soldiers shot and died at long range. They were ferocious episodes of close combat where generals fought personally in the front line and led on their troops to cut through the flesh and bone of individual opponents. Alexander had inherited his father's balanced battle-formation, but its distinctive units of infantry, armed with very long spears, had never been recreated since their final defeat by Roman soldiers in 167 BC. For the past two thousand years their manoeuvres had survived only in the ancients' own subsequent text-books. Somehow, the drill would have to be reinvented and the stars would have to learn to fight hand-to-hand, often from horseback without stirrups.

Unless these battles could give a real impression of the Macedonians' formations in action, they would spread a totally false image of how Alexander conquered so much of the world. In Oliver's previous experience there was only one candidate for the role of military director: Captain Dale Dye, formerly of the American marines and since 1985 the head of Warriors Incorporated.

Now aged 58, Dale Dye's film career had grown up with Oliver's, extending right back to their staging of the powerful scenes of Vietnam warfare in 'Platoon'. It was Dale Dye who trained the American troops for Oliver's 'Born on the Fourth of July' and in the mid-1990's for 'Heaven and Earth'. It was Dale Dye who trained Mickey and Mallory, Oliver's two 'Natural Born Killers', in their uncanny use of weaponry. Twenty years on set and greying hair had not dimmed his upright military presence, complete with baton, combat jacket and trousers and a rich line in expletives. On 'Platoon', the cast had characterised him and Oliver as John Wayne and Ho Chi Minh respectively. "The only thing that has changed", Dale Dye assured me, "is that Oliver has shifted to the right."

Like the stars, I was introduced to the Captain by telephone two months before training was to begin. "The name's Dye, Captain Dale Dye of Warriors Incorporated", the firm American accent told me on the answer-phone one July evening. "Oliver Stone is seconding you to my army, so ring me and we'll discuss what's involved". What was involved, initially, was a verbal dressing-down from a veteran ex-Marine who certainly did not spare his vocabulary. "Hi, Doc", the voice answered me, "Oliver's landed me with every slimeball and maggot in the Western hemisphere, but I want you to know that there's no bigger slimeball than a Professor from Oxford University. You may think you can ride, and you may want to act as a soldier. But in my unit, you aren't *acting* as a soldier, you're going to learn how to *be* a soldier. You're not coming here to be some left-leaning, bum-pinching commie. You'll have to be broken down before you can be built up. You're going to want to die for your country, because your country ain't going to be saved, unless people go on dying for it, whether you're a Macedonian on screen or an American out in a foxhole. Doc, do you even know what a foxhole is?" I have to say that over here, we call them foxes' earths, I corrected him, thinking of my happy hunting days in English woodlands. The voice on the telephone groaned in disgust. Dale regarded me as one more challenge, among the hundreds which 'Alexander' had already landed on him. But there was something about his voice which recognised the humour and humanity of the situation. Over the next eight months, scores of us were to find the same.

Dale Dye had soldiered, with decorations, in Vietnam; he had soldiered in Nicaragua and elsewhere in central America; in 1985, on the edge of his forties, he had retired back to California and had formed 'Warriors Incorporated' in the hope of upping Hollywood's style of war-games on screen. It was a remote hope. "War movies pissed me off", he told me later, at a relaxed midday meeting on location. "The weapon-handling was all wrong, the tactical details were all wrong; the soldiers were film-stars, not soldiers". Movies were breeding their own conventions of what 'historical' fighting looked like: a swipe from side to side with a mace or a sword was followed by a clatter on a shield, no tension, no strain

A bloodied Ptolemy (Elliot Cowan) attacks with his sword as the cavalry collide with their Indian enemies.

Alexander (Colin Farrell), Cassander (Jonathan Rhys Meyers), Hephaestion (Jared Leto) and Craterus (Rory McCann) catch sight of the women in the Harem at Babylon.

A jubilant army welcome Alexander, recovered from his wound in the Indian elephant battle.

and no battle-energy. The film-makers were all "too conceited to want to return and learn from the military". Hollywood had its own stereotype of soldiers: "toothless brutes from the South."

The Captain certainly still has teeth, though when I first met him he had shaved the bushy white cavalry moustache which would make a return appearance for the cavalry battle in 'India'. Films, Dale Dye has always insisted, "have a very big impact on youth, but the youth of the audiences is not a constant thing. The least that film-battles should aim for is that the viewers should suspend disbelief." But that suspension has become very difficult. Since the late 1960's documentaries and television have been showing footage of live action in real wars. They edit out most of the violence, but the images have made Hollywood's traditional slash and bash style even more artificial. The result is that during battle-scenes, the younger audiences disconnect. The battles break the spell. "Sod it", the Captain decided, "I'll fix it". He founded Warriors Inc. in order to bring film-fighting back to a level which would seem convincing.

At first, it seemed a hopeless struggle. The big directors had enough to worry about already in the awkward name of 'authenticity'. "Why do we need you, Dale?": let film-battles be film-battles, and let the actors continue to be trained to what their audiences are used to seeing. It would go on, Hollywood style, but "we'll call you, Captain, if we have problems about the choice of buttons for the uniforms".

In a film-trade paper, Dale Dye then read that a young, untried American director was trying to raise funding for a film about the war in Vietnam which would show it through the eyes of a group of ordinary American soldiers. Like Dale, the director Oliver Stone was a Vietnam war-veteran himself and on their first meeting, the two of them found they shared a rapport and an objective. Oliver explained that he wanted his actors in 'Platoon' 'to go out on set with some sort of training in the strains and hardships of a real Vietnam platoon. As a result, he and Dale Dye took them off for a fortnight to an island in the south Philippines where they were equipped with shovels and told to dig their own holes in the rock-hard ground at nightfall. The handles of the shovels broke, the stars' hands blistered and as they tried to bed down in their shallow apologies for foxholes, Dale gave them an authentic army welcome. Simulated mortar-fire and shells burst round them all night from their enemy's general direction. For the next two weeks, the barrage continued and nobody slept for more than two and a half hours a night. On the final morning, a dazed Platoon was taken straight from their random horror at 6 am and made to begin filming on set at 9:30 am. It is no wonder that the actors had the look of dazed exhaustion and nervous fatigue which Oliver wanted, the Vietnam emotions which he had lived out in real life.

Alexander's army, I reflected thankfully, had never had to dig themselves in and as a cavalryman, I would be spared the attempt to dig my own (Lane) Foxhole. A month later, when I met the Captain in his office at Pinewood studios, I had no idea of what ground he was already covering between three countries. Out in his Californian orchard, Colin was already learning to absorb the Captain's idea of the battle of Gaugamela's formations. "What you are seeing here", Dale Dye had told a recording-team from Diverse Productions, who had come to film the process, "is the first unscrewing and turning of his head: he has to think like Alexander, until he senses and feels it as second nature". Colin was certainly sensing and feeling, and perhaps he was still repeating 'Jedd', the Captain's memory-key for leadership, while moving the pieces around on his table of the battle.

Out in Morocco, meanwhile, arrangements were being finalised for the use of about a thousand soldiers on the Lakhfaouna desert location. The King of Morocco's personal approval had helped to arrange that most of them would first attend one of Dale's celebrated 'boot-camps'. For years, since boyhood, Dale Dye had read about Alexander's campaigns and admired his military genius. Since joining the Alexander project, he had gone through some of the scholarly handbooks on the Macedonian army and read a selection of the ancient texts in translation. He had worked out a manageable formation in which to 'mousetrap' and neutralize the scythed chariots which were to be launched by the enemy Persian army. He had specified the very different weaponry, including body-length shields, which was to be used by the varied ethnic units of the Persian King's opposing troops. Since 'Platoon', Warriors Inc. have recreated eighteenth-century battles; they also staged the fighting for 'Band of Brothers' and 'Saving Private Ryan'. But ancient history was about two thousand years removed from anything they had done before. For the first time, Dale himself would be a Unit Director, directing the filming on the second of the two battle-units into which Oliver had separated the desert-filming in order to keep up with the schedule.

When we met in Pinewood, a month before boot-camp, there were visible signs of months of pre-planning but, personally, I underestimated them. In a corner of his sparse office, the Captain had placed his back-pack, ready for rapid action, and a menacing pair of weights, for training and keeping fit. On the walls were pinned the photographs of his key army personnel, the celebrated Dale's Core, men with names like Billy Budd or Colin's cavalry trainer, Freddie Joe. "Over the years," Dale told me "I have picked up hard men I can trust, and when we have a job we ring them up". They looked to my eye like a Wanted List of thieves from either side of the Atlantic, with only one woman amongst them: Julia Rapkalvis, Vice-President of Warriors Inc.. Julia holds a Doctorate in Theatrical Hoplology from Union Institute, Cincinnati, Ohio: 'hoplology' is formed from two ancient Greek words and means the 'theory of weapons'. She also has a rock-hard reputation for single combat. As the Executive Director of the Society of American Fight Directors, she is the one woman who could wrestle with Colin Farrell and not fall voluntarily over backwards. "She is as tough as nails", a chastened Colin later admitted, "but always cares what happens". Out by his Californian caravan, while Dale and I met, she was teaching him how to grapple hand to hand and to slash a hanging water melon with a swipe of his sword, as if slicing off an enemy's neck.

For the foot units, Dale Dye had done his homework. The centre of Alexander's infantry line was the famous infantry phalanx whose weaponry was so distinctive. With both hands, each soldier held a long pike, or sarissa, about eighteen feet long, tipped with a spear blade and at the other end, a metal butt-spike. The 'sarissas' of the front four ranks would project out beyond the formation's front line: their length kept the enemy at bay, like a boxer who was gifted with a much longer reach than his opponent. When the men marched, the effect was like a mobile 'hedgehog' bristling with spears. If necessary, the unit could halt and the back ranks could face about and the soldiers on the end of each line could face sideways. The phalanx then became a set square bristling with pikes, or sarissas, projecting in all four directions.

How on earth were modern infantrymen to manoeuvre in this formation, wearing mass-produced armour and no covering on their upper legs? How could they avoid poking the ranks behind with their butt-spikes? The Captain had read details from ancient military manuals describing the 'locked shield' manoeuvre, when the phalanx soldiers drilled tightly together, leaving only a metre between each man: he had studied the more open formations when, apparently, the troops wheeled and turned briskly. We know that Alexander's phalanx was drawn up at varying depths, 32 ranks, 16 or (for his big victory at Issus in 333BC) only 8 ranks deep. The basic unit appeared to be based on the number 16, although Macedonians remained attached to a notional 'decad', or unit of ten. The ancient manuals which were written a century or more after Alexander's death described a core unit of 16 by 16, 256 men in all. It was this unit which Dale Dye adopted and described by the ancient Greek name, syntagma.

With a syntagma as his building block, the Captain could figure out possible ways of manoeuvring obliquely to the right or to the left. 'Wheeling' and facing about would be slow with inexperienced soldiers, but by moving obliquely across open ground, the phalanx, he reasoned, could eventually 'drift' right or left-handed without splitting. Extra blocks, or syntagmata, of 256 could be added as necessary, bulking up the unit as circumstances required. Above all, the basic unit of 16 appealed to the Captain's own military experience. It made up the 'platoon'-sized unit of each Macedonian's battle-life: the members were the people he fought and died for, and the men next to him were the people who really motivated him. The syntagma gave the phalanx flexibility, but it also gave it cohesion, loyalty and strength.

To Dale Dye's mind, the phalanx had the qualities of a modern tank corps. It moved slowly and inexorably, sweeping away the enemy in front of it, or else it stood firm and made an essential anchor for Alexander's entire line. A rock firm centre, in Dale Dye's opinion, was the key to victory. Ancient sources and historians like myself emphasise the shock force of Alexander's cavalry charges, but the Captain, a lifelong foot soldier, is sceptical. "You guys are sexually stimulated by careering about on horseback; forget it. What won these battles was an infantry which could not be broken open and, if it split, one which could reform and stand firm in smaller units". To anchor it more firmly, its right flank was linked up with the finest infantry troops in all history, the toughened Shield Bearers whom Alexander inherited from his father Philip. By the time they reached India, many of these deadly armoured fighters were over sixty years old. If the phalanx started to drift, the elderly Shield Bearers were there on the right of it to hold it firm. They were its link with the cavalry, "sexually stimulated" or not, and they were its guard against an enemy's outflanking movements into its right side.

Big battles in films like 'Gladiator' have only been based on their directors' fantasy and free imagination. The opening battle in that film was widely admired, but its Roman soldiers' tactic of filling trenches with fire was pointed out, before filming, to be ungrounded in evidence, a fantasy of the directorial team which they insisted upon, nonetheless. There was no basic fantasy about Oliver and Dale Dye's phalanx: it was solidly based on history. As seen on screen, the core units, filmed in the desert, have been multiplied by 'visual effects' and given a second reserve line, as the ancient histories of the battle describe. But the core of it all is a real cluster of syntagmata, who had been drilling and toiling in the desert while the cavalry raised huge clouds of dust on their flanks, something which no technique could ever simulate, no more than it could have simulated the human tension and violence which make the 'Alexander' battles so spellbinding.

When we met in Pinewood, Dale Dye had already mapped out his battle-plan on his computer. On it we could see the phalanx parting ranks to 'mousetrap' a Persian chariot; he had been able at his desk to simulate the 'obliques' which were such an important part of his thinking. In the ancients' histories, I asked him, surely the Persian scythed chariots careered through the parted ranks of Macedonian infantry, but the infantry threw javelins at some of them and hurled their drivers off the platforms as they passed? Is the 'mousetrap' historically attested? Years of dealing with a Press Corps has made the Captain hyper-sceptical: "Whatever the writers said afterwards", he answered, "how on earth did they know? The truth is they didn't. They made it up. War correspondents make it up, and those guys, Arrian and Plutarch and Curtius, weren't even in the battle or alive within three centures of the event". True, they themselves were not, but their underlying sources were, so far as they could see any of the action unfolding. But in Dale Dye's view, we have to interpret, both because we do not really know the truth and because we cannot train soldiers for the twenty years which Philip imposed on his men before Alexander led them to war. We can take a historically grounded framework, keep the sarissas, the cavalry charges, the Shield Bearers, but all too often, he feels, academics start insisting on what are only their half-supported guesses anyway. As a result, 'professionals' are such a pain on set. "When some war historian starts trying to tell me 'It's generally accepted', the alarm-bells start ringing in my head. I've read your account of Gaugamela, and half a dozen others, but it doesn't make sense; none of you have tried to do what you describe, and most of these 'classical studies' are bullshit, or based on it. When you've done it, I'll believe you - and I figure that if Dale Dye can do it, then Alexander of Macedon certainly could do it too. We'll see".

There were still plenty of imponderables: armed with sarissas, how fast could untrained men move before they split ranks? How high would the sarissas of the central ranks have to be held in order to keep clear of those in front and to break the flight of any missiles which Oliver launched at them? Nobody knew, because nobody had seen a full phalanx in action since Macedon's defeat by Rome in the mid-second century BC. I did not see any point in observing that the syntagma and the number 256 are attested only in ancient text books writen long after Alexander's lifetime when the system might have changed. How did we know it had (or hadn't), or was I just one more example of those 'academic weenies' whom the Captain believed he could refute by practical experiments in the desert?

In Alexander's phalanx, we do at least know that the front line and the back line troops were eventually paid extra and were particularly esteemed. Now I realised why: they had been 'Alexander's Core'. On the walls of the Captain's office, 'Dale's Core' looked chunkily down at us, faces with names like Mike Stokey or the visually named Toad. The cavalry, on the whole, was not so central to the Captain's thinking. The cavalry fieldcommander was to be Warrant Officer Farnsworth, the Freddie Joe who was still working on Colin's riding skills in California. The Captain himself was not getting on a horse, though he would try sitting on a camel.

For Alexander's horsemen, two cavalry formations are attested in the texts. The ancient historians talk of a wedge shape, like a sharply pointed triangle, for the crucial breakthrough by Alexander's cavalry on the right wing of the battle. Dale Dye, however, felt that the diamond (which is better known for troops on Alexander's left wing) would be visually more distinct and much easier to manoeuvre in our all-important 'left turn' against the Persian centre. The man on the left point of the diamond would lead the way by turning left, while the men at the diamond's head would then wheel round to fit in behind him. It would do near enough, if, that is, we could do it at all, with stars who had only ridden for a month and would have to go bareback, with Colin who had last been seen on screen on a motorbike and among the Moroccans, a natural-born shirker from Oxford, myself, and a cluster of Dale's Core who looked likely to be more at home with a mortar-bomb than a bit in a horse's mouth.

If we ever went on to Thailand, the Indian battle would be less structured. The essence of it would be for Alexander's troops to be thrown into confusion and to begin to hang back, alarmed at the sight of war-elephants, a weapon which Hollywood had never deployed, let alone against horsemen. There was plenty of scope for the desired effect of terror, chaos and vengeance in what the Captain graphically described as a 'clusterf***'. We could probably cluster and come up with one, but Gaugamela had to be a victory with a coordinated plan, one which a film audience could understand. For precisely that reason, there was to be Dale Dye's boot camp. As the Captain told me when we re-met in Morocco, "Doc, always remember there's no problem in life which can't be solved by a dose of high explosive".

Alexander (Colin Farrell) exhorts his troops before Gaugamela.

The Persian chariots and army prepare for battle at Gaugamela.

Oliver Stone and Alexander (Colin Farrell) discuss a last minute script direction before the phalanx at Gaugamela.

12. In the Boot Camp

A boot camp is an intense session of military training, but it has become a widely accepted preparation for an action movie since the mid-1980's and Oliver Stone's 'Platoon'. The public image of a Hollywood star as a spoilt, overpaid idler does not take these camps into account. Colin Farrell had already gone through one, for 11 days of action before his lead part in 'Tigerland'. He knew what to expect in Morocco and was looking forward to it. The male parts in Alexander would be totally impossible for actors who wanted to sit in a hotel room and complain all day about their hairstyles.

It was not, as participants sometimes moaned, that Dale and Oliver, two Vietnam veterans, were wanting to impose what they themselves had undergone onto younger men who were about to play soldiers at their direction. Actors come into a film from all sorts of backgrounds, with no experience of each other and no real idea of the army or the action which they are trying to represent. In his boot camps, Dale Dye insists that actors call each other only by their script names, never by their personal names. Boot camp sets the stars apart from their previous style of life, a real 'rite of passage' from one form of life into another. Rites of passage have been widely studied in remote cultures which are even more exotic or primitive than Hollywood's. But in a film like 'Alexander', they are alive and kicking at the centre of western entertainment.

By early September, campsites near the Moroccan desert location had been set aside for 17 days' military training. Anyone who was cast for a main military part was obliged to participate, and by now other 'possibles' had dropped off the list, even when they had gone as far as a trial costume-fitting. Talk of muscle-building and a few frank phrases from Captain Dye had prompted second thoughts. The survivors were all enthusiastic. For Jared Leto, boot-camp would be a good challenge after a while away from film roles. Elliot Cowan was coming fresh from the theatre where boot-camps were completely out of the question; the older recruits were undeterred, even those, like Dale Dye, who were on the wrong side of fifty. The mature John Kavanagh, playing Parmenion, had some idea of what to expect from his role in 'Braveheart' and the bulky Brian Blessed could also be counted on, at this stage cast as the important phalanx commander, Coenus.

There were two exceptions: eunuchs and Oxford professors. In August, Oliver had still been talking of my 'putting on some muscle', but Dale Dye was satisfied that foxhunting qualified me as a competent rider and anyway, I was entirely dispensable if the role proved too much. Pleading the pressure of work, I went peacefully off to Italy to look at art instead. There was also a let out for the star dancer, Francisco Bosch, who was playing Bagoas the Persian eunuch. Oliver had threatened him with boot-camp too, but weapon-training was not exactly relevant to his unmilitary role. As the one recruit from a ballet corps, he already had muscles which were more than adequate.

Between late August and mid-September every other man on screen in the Gaugamela scenes was out under canvas, learning to be tough and competent. At the time of Gaugamela (in 331BC) Alexander's army had three years of victories in Asia already behind them and up to twenty years of previous training with Philip. It was Philip, I now realised, who had actually invented the idea of 'boot-camp' in the first place. Philip recruited Macedonian men into his kingdom's first-ever royal standing army and obliged them to go on long forced marches of 35 miles or more and to learn to carry heavy packs of tents and up to 30 days' rations of flour on their backs. Washing in hot water was forbidden in his Macedonia, people said, even for any woman who had just given birth. This rule did not seem too relevant when 'Alexander's' boot-camp began.

Dale Dye embarked on it with various aims. He wanted his film-commanders to gain a fuller experience of the units they would be leading on screen. He wanted his own warriors in 'Dale's Core' to learn the historical Macedonian tactics and to help to hold together the Moroccans and others in the big units who would be learning them for the first time. Drilling would be imperative if the phalanx manoeuvres, including the 'mousetrap', were ever to be effective. Close up, the individuals' skills of combat would need toughening, not least by his hoplologist, Julia. The horsemen could be handed over to Freddie Joe and the horsemasters, but above all, a random group of prima donnas must be bonded and brought under Colin's example as leader.

In Dale Dye's experience, film battles work best when the actors "learn to be larger than themselves". The problem is that in an actor's life, there is nothing else so large. They all arrive wanting to be movie stars, not actors, but the Captain's reaction is "no, turd, you're a soldier". In boot camp, they discover that "the sun doesn't rise or set on their arse". One of Dale's rallying calls is "leave that Hollywood crap behind you". Another is "don't say 'please' or 'sorry' or 'thank you'". The style of command must be clear-cut: "I bark, and you jump". But "in order to lead men, you also have to love them". Colin was already shaping up well here, after those weeks with Jedd and the twigs and bottle caps. The need was to rid all the others of their "internalised emotional baggage". After a day or two, they might start wondering exactly who was the one with the baggage to lose, but Dale's method stays rock hard: "make them, or break them, and the only way is to press the bastards". If you want a savagely commited bulldog, the answer (in Dale's view) is not to feed it.

In none of his many boot-camps has anyone yet walked out on him: participants often like to feel themselves changing. 'Method acting' is a major part of the experience. On Alexander, it meant a simulation of Dale's view of ancient soldiering. There was to be nothing to eat for breakfast, a minimal lunch of fruit, nuts and cheese, no mobile phones, no Christian names, a first meal of the day in the evening, only two or three showers to a unit, primitive latrines and no women, except for Julia and a gorgeous stunt-coordinator, with occasional glimpses of Rosario (Roxane) to keep up the pressure during rehearsals. In the hot sun, there was soon an unexpected bonus: maggots were found squirming in the bowls of lunchtime nuts. Water was freely available, but there was no alcohol and no cigarettes and one of the main sports in the evening was staging races between the dung beetles which had been caught from the latrine trenches. Above all there was physical exercise, starting after no breakfast and continuing in the full desert heat of 40-45°C after next to no lunch. Wake-up, or reveille, was at 6am: "get up, you turds". Within an hour, the four 'syntagmata' of troops would be out in the desert for the daily morning run. As the sun gained heat, Dale Dye would lead them across five or six kilometers of desert, singing company-songs as they ran. "Mama, Mama, can't you see What Alexander's done to me?…": the actors increasingly improvised their own brutal versions. What happened, I wondered, if you had a bad stomach? "Easy", Perdiccas (Neil Jackson) told me, "you just ran faster."

After the running, it would be time for Physical Training (including press-ups) and then the fighting. Dale's Core includes former Royal Marines, chunky individuals who are more than willing to challenge a film-star head on. There was also Julia to be reckoned with, a self-styled Dialogue Coach for the body. Killing, she insists, should never be the main aim of battle. Gaining ground is much more important and in her view, the greatest armies are those with a sense of this greater goal. In order to attain it, the boot-campers needed to learn swordplay (a turn with a steel sword would teach them to appreciate its weight). They also needed to learn to sling missiles, an art in which some of them soon nicknamed their own particular styles (the 'Elvis'; the 'double doughnut').

For the first five days it seemed as if Dale Dye was one of the enemy, dressed in his short-sleeved shirt with a message saying 'Pain is Weakness Leaving the Body'. Mistakes or insubordination were greeted with "Drop me twenty!" (twenty press-ups in the heat). But they were all in it together, whatever the size of their role, their contract or their payment. Naturally, the others looked to Colin for a lead and were reassured by what they found: somebody who had a kind word for all of them and, already a true Alexander, who would never let something difficult be demanded of others without promptly demanding it of himself.

Riding practice, without stirrups, had already begun for the main cavalry officers and was being held every afternoon under the masterly guidance of the horsemaster Ricardo Cruz Moral and his Spanish team. The horses varied, or was it their riders? Despite his Irish roots, Jonathan Rhys Meyers never really took to the bareback cavalry action and was content to give way to his double. Gary Stretch, as Cleitus, had a lovely grey horse and somehow, his professional boxer's physique seemed to settle easily onto it. As Hephaestion, Jared Leto quickly emerged as a surprise horseman in the making, his long legs untroubled by his horse's fidgeting. Colin had already picked up the knack, after his weeks in Spain and California. For Ptolemy (Elliot Cowan) it was more of a battle. He began with two heavy falls and on a day of dark storm clouds, he found his horse, Ramadan, was unusually nervous. After falling again, he went off and found himself weeping with frustration: "I'll never ride the bugger…". But like the weather, the bugger settled down and Ptolemy emerged with an elegant style of control. Unexpectedly, the most experienced horseman was the actor who only had to ride once, when entering Babylon: Ian Beattie, playing Antigonus on foot, is the Irish son of a circus-artist. From the age of seven, he had ridden daily, even learning how to stand up on a horse's back. In the most thorough biography of their Director there are photographs of the young Oliver on horseback, with stirrups. It was probably just as well that the stars had not seen them and were not trying to copy the positioning of his legs.

For the first days in boot-camp, the focus was on the generals-to-be, Colin, the Silver Shields and the main Companions. "I told you, you were going to hit walls," the Captain warned them, "and if you answer back, you go home". A few days in, and Brian Blessed was forced to go home anyway: he suffered a hernia after a hard day of running and physical working out. With him went a big part for Coenus who, in history, had voiced the discontents of the weary Macedonian army in India. Brian, typically, would be back on the Pinewood set three months later in a physically demanding role: he was recast as the tough Leonidas, the young Macedonians' wrestling trainer. By a quick shift of parts, the big speech for Coenus in India went to Rory McCann, indestructibly tall and fit from his years in Scotland's forests.

After the running and exercise, the morning would be spent in hand-to -hand fighting or in supervised sessions of sword-on-shield combat. "Break down your opponent's territorial imperatives," Dale and his Core kept telling the stars, "get in close up, get used to being too near to each other". Maggots followed for lunch, and then there would be a bit more fighting, with a session on horses and a trip up to Oliver's tent at base camp for reading-rehearsals, scene by scene. Once again, the stars were impressed by Oliver's detailed involvement with their acting. Before long, the team were rehearsing the Wedding Scene and having a first encounter with Roxane (Rosario). To her female eye, the camp was clearly all about boy-bonding: she quickly noticed how the men actors, always the copycats, were almost all covered in tattoos, their fashion-statements. To them, she seemed like a torment from the world outside camp. As Perdiccas (Neil Jackson) recalls, the rehearsing was very intense, even for those on the margins of a scene. While Colin is being lured to marry Rosario, the other officers have to sit and grumble, but Oliver was not letting anyone be apathetic, on or off camera. "What is Perdiccas thinking all the time?" he would force Neil to think, "Don't just stare and sit back. Why is he standing beside Cleitus? What are you thinking about Hephaestion? Clarify the relationships and keep them tight". The drama, the actors learned, did not stop with the couple who were centre-stage: "In Alexander's last days is Perdiccas thinking of killing Alexander? Relate to him," Oliver kept urging, "and keep on showing it".

Back in camp, mundane tasks were everyone's tasks. It was for each tent group to start up a fire (preferably without modern matches), to keep it burning, to go on collecting firewood, to cook, to wash up. Each person must be responsible for his own kit and tent-space. They were sleeping on slats ten to a tent, one Moroccan to nine outsiders: as in Alexander's army, cavalry men were quartered with cavalry, infantrymen with infantry. But whatever their rank, they were all treated alike, from Alexander down to phalanx-

The Macedonian and Indian armies engage ferociously on foot in the Indian elephant battle.

Pre-production drawing for a wall 'mosaic' in Ptolemy's study in Alexandria, showing Alexander attacking elephants in India.

An emotional Alexander (Colin Farrell) surveys the dead on the Gaugamela battlefield.

Pre-production drawing of Alexander's army camp by night.

material like Dick Crowley, a personal friend since schooldays of co-producer Jon Kilik who had kindly had him cast in the infantry and then put into boot-camp as a change from his life in the construction business in Arizona.

Each night, after a dinner of stew, the Captain would lecture crisply and clearly on the Macedonian army, the thinking behind it and the tactics ahead of the actors and extras. His audience found these evening 'stand downs' the high point of the day, and not only because of what had gone before. Dale Dye is a practised communicator since his army training in handling a press corps. He spoke of the greatness of Alexander's father Philip, "the founder of modern warfare", who had trained a battle-line which was intelligently varied and, most importantly, balanced. Alexander had then made a fluid use of the units which he inherited, moving them around for each battle like pieces on a chessboard. Dale Dye stressed, correctly, Alexander's ability to "synthesise a situation" and to react ingeniously to new terrains and new styles of enemy fighting: his victories were not won by mindless force. With hindsight, as old Ptolemy remembers in the film, we can see the huge risks which Alexander took. But he did not waver, and he won. In Dale's view, Alexander had an acute sense of "spatial geometry".

There was also Alexander's famous gift for leadership which he had developed from Philip's example. Dale Dye's own years of military experiences made him unusually sceptical of something which armchair historians stress: the importance of Alexander's personal 'spell' as battle was about to begin. Do we really even know that Alexander always fought in the very front rank, Dale Dye put it to me? I would say 'certainly' because of the surviving ancient texts and his well attested list of broken bones and wounds. "But were the historians telling the truth?", Dale persisted. In my view, they certainly were, but Dale's view is that even if they were (for him, unlikely), Alexander's heroics would be pretty much irrelevant to ordinary soldiers as a battle loomed. Achilles, Zeus, the god Dionysus: "so what? A soldier will never bet on a mythical horse". But what about the speeches which Alexander gave before battle? In four weeks' time, in the first action scene to be filmed, Colin would have to harangue the troops while galloping on his big black horse and to urge them, on the desert battlefield, to fight for such ideals as 'glory' and 'the Greeks'. A bit of Alexander's speech at this time is even preserved for us in the version of his personal publicist. Nonetheless, historians argue whether the record of such speeches is simply fiction and the speeches would have been inaudible; what does the Captain think? "He can shout out whatever he likes, but what matters - and Alexander understood this - is what the unit and platoon-commanders then say to the small groups of soldiers within the line". Sure enough, the best surviving ancient narrative, by Arrian, does describe how Alexander summoned his generals before Gaugamela and explained that he would not be making long speeches: it was for the unit and squad-commanders to exhort the men under their command. Historians tend to pass over this fact, but Dale Dye made me notice it.

Why, indeed, did the Macedonians go on fighting? They were trained to it; they were loyal to their king; they took plunder galore, over and above their pay. From India onwards, it seems that they also fell heavily into debt, run up with traders, presumably, who were servicing them during the march: 'Alexander' crew-members who fell behind

115

with their hotel bills could easily sympathise. If a soldier-debtor then tried to desert, his creditor (perhaps one of his officers) would be able to enslave him. "Nonsense," Dale Dye snorted, "they were not simply in it for the money; you can't run an army by debt. What kept those guys going was that the experience made them feel they were somebody. They mattered, they were important for the first time. The crowds had gaped at them as they entered a vast place like Babylon, far bigger than any city they'd ever seen. What did these soldiers have at home? A sagging wife and a few sheep. Soldiers love to win, and to boast about their exploits. Through Alexander, they had pride in themselves". Certainly, in Alexander's lifetime, we start to have sketches in Greek comic plays of 'boastful soldiers' who are returning from the East. Dale Dye would understand the truth behind these new 'castings' in Greek drama. The last thing that most Macedonian veterans wanted to do was to retire: the veterans mutinied when Alexander tried to send them home in 324 BC: they returned after his death and fought on, like Oliver's old-age fighters, though many of them were well over sixty.

Dale Dye lectured his recruits that they were "attempting to do something which had not been done for 2000 years". Certainly, nobody had ever recreated the tactics of the Macedonian phalanx, but what about the camping and the lack of breakfast? One of the greatest modern Alexander-historians, Helmut Berve, wrote page after page on the organization and infra-structure of Alexander's army in the first volume of his book on the 'Alexanderreich', composed in the Germany of the 1920's. Sanitation and 'care' were all covered in thorough detail, but even Berve could find next to no ancient evidence and as the headings were based on his own orderly notions, they now seem rather odd . We do not happen to hear of breakfast on Alexander's march, but that is probably because the surviving sources are so defective on the whole topic: they never tell us what Alexander's troops usually ate, although grain and fruit were surely their staples. Meat was not a part of a Greek's usual diet, except such meat as was distributed at a religious sacrifice or caught as game while hunting. However, there were probably times when Alexander's army ate the sheep and livestock which were driven off as plunder and herded along with the army and so Dale's diet of nuts, fruit and evening stew was not too wide of the mark. Of the Macedonian latrines, we know nothing, although the boot-camp proved that 50-120,000 men would have encouraged a vast number of dung beetles.

The boot-camp routine, then, was not a sadistic invention: it hurt, because the participants had not had long years of practice with King Philip. But did two aims become confused? The crucial aim was to practise and train the unfamiliar tactics: would the ranks have been more capable of drilling if they were being better fed? Recently-retired British marines in the corps did also wonder if the 'bark, and jump' style of command was necessarily Alexander's: in British camps, this style has been moderated since the 1970's, in favour of a lower-key psychological approach. Unlike the men in boot-camp, Alexander's men did have the women whom they had collected, even 'married', on the march. But here, the boot-camp had a second, important aim: to put the team through an ordeal, so as to bond them and knock the 'Hollywood' out of them. How did it seem to participants?

Ian Beattie had been cast as a tough old infantry officer, Antigonus the One-Eyed, a veteran of Philip's years of campaigning. Ian had just come off the film 'Women's Pirates', where he had been playing a drug-dealer, and after a brief rest in his native Belfast, he had come south for the part which would be such a big break. In fact, we only know that Antigonus was with Alexander's army for a few months: he stayed back on the Asian coast for an important role behind the main front. As a historian I had tried to have him written out of the battle-scripts, but Oliver already had Ian in mind, and he liked the 'one-eyed' image. So Antigonus acquired an unattested career. On arrival in boot-camp, Ian was leaving behind his fiancée Michelle, a dear step-son and his own recently-born son Jimmy. To amuse them he kept a diary.

At first, it all seemed like a dream come true. He freely invited his fellow-stars to his forthcoming wedding: it was sad not to be able to phone home but "I am so incredibly lucky - me here, with Colin who's such a great guy to us and Oliver, a genius in the world... I also feel myself getting fitter and starting to lose weight. I have started to do extra sit-ups over the last few days and to lose the last bicycle-tyre on me. But I miss the two boys back home so much...". The only ominous development was the presence of scorpions in camp and the frequency of scorpion bites through the open-laced military boots.

By the second day, as Dale Dye had warned them, it seemed so much more difficult. "Oh Christ, I am going to die: I am almost a celebrity, but get me out of here...". In Ian's case, the camp became particularly painful. During the first close-combat session, he had tried to run at one of the toughest hunks in Dale's Core (the ex-army Brit, who had the nickname 'Toad'). 'Antigonus's' attempt caused Toad to butt him with his head, leaving Ian in need of stitches in his left cheek. Dale Dye at once offered him a way-out to a surgery, but Ian was not giving up: "I'll die first," he told the Captain, "here in camp and you'll carry my cold dead body back to the hospital before I leave". So a Moroccan doctor came out to attend to him, but as Ian sat, he saw that Colin had promptly stood up to be the next man to take on 'Toad'. 'Alexander' was leading, sure enough, by example.

Within hours, Antigonus the One-Eyed risked becoming Antigonus the One-Cheeked. The Moroccan doctor insisted on putting stitches in the wound, and yet Ian, in boot-camp spirit, refused flatly to have an anaesthetic. Three stitches went in, perhaps as they might have done two thousand years ago, but during the night, one of them broke loose, and so a doctor was brought back to pull the old thread out and put a new thread in. Still without an anaesthetic, Ian found the doctor apologising for his slowness and muttering that he was half-asleep. But the stitches held good: it was Colin, typically, who had seen to the ice-packs, as he continued to do for anyone who was sprained or strained.

On Day Five, the generals noticed how Dale Dye was now swinging firmly behind them, a sign of his approval at their acceptance of the initial breaking-down. The troops were split into four companies, named after ancient Greek letters of the alphabet, Alpha, Beta, Gamma, Sigma, and 250 or so of the Moroccan soldiers had now joined the training. But the pace did not exactly ease up. "Sunday 7th Sept: it is 6am, and no day of rest here. But breakfast was served: one slice of bread, thank you. Phalanx training followed the hardest run and training exercise so far: probably it was to break in the Moroccans". 'Beta' course (Ian's unit) came third out of three. "Hell, I hate losing". Like Ian, the actors were becoming highly competitive over almost anything, over their fighting, their drilling, their running and even such things as their cooking and making fires. "Sunday a day of rest? My arse. They took us out for three hours in the roasting sun on phalanx manoeuvres - a tough hot day for the Moroccans, but they have a great spirit". The officers were now regularly shouting the drill-orders to big infantry groups in formation, and as the Moroccan numbers grew, interpreters had to translate for them. There is still some dispute over the means by which Alexander's foot soldiers received orders, but Dale Dye was surely right to use standard-bearers who could signal with banners beside the main unit. Trumpeters were also used by Alexander's army, so Dale added them to the "stop-go" signalling. They used long trumpets which the props team had drawn as straight ones, not the curved horns which are known in the Roman era.

During the day, words like "scumbag" now circulated freely and the officers played to their respective strengths. Relationships between them started to reflect their relationships in the film-script, with a similar sense that Colin, though on for everything, was always slightly apart. The Captain had quickly cast the main Englishman, Elliot Cowan, in a sort of English 'Sandhurst officer' role and Elliot recycled bits of his past theatre-training. "All I want is a proper cup of coffee, made in a proper copper coffee pot", Elliot recited in the early morning, repeating a training-sentence from English drama-school. Before long, Dale Dye would be repeating it among the more usual barrage of "Take me to hell and high water... drop me twenty... I love this crap".

In the evenings, by the camp fire, there was music and singing, enhanced by the Moroccan soldiers who camped apart, but sang heartily and danced under the stars. The young Alexander, young Connor Paolo, came down to join in these campfire evenings and already alarmed the rest of the cast by his assured cool and premature know-how. The singing would bring Oliver down too, enjoying the unexpected gusto with which his Irish casting could keep up the tempo, as if it was a really enjoyable life. "Day 9: at training this morning we repulsed a cavalry charge and learned how to 'mousetrap' a chariot...". In the evening "Irish songs to Oliver...Oliver wants people to improve: no problem about that, anyway". But the strain was telling too: "people are dropping now like flies".

As the second week began, the main actors were up at Oliver's rehearsal tent when Colin received some specially exciting news: back in California his girlfriend, Kim, had given birth to their baby boy. Rehearsals were stopped for some celebratory champagne, the first alcohol for more than ten days. From a dark sky, a giant shower of hailstones, as big as golf balls, marked the occasion, followed by heavy rain which caused mud and puddles. Stripping down, Colin went out in his underpants to roll in the mud as a celebration. Alexander, too, had had a first son by his Persian mistress Barsine and had called him 'Heracles'. But King Philip would not have allowed even Kim a bath in warm water: out in Morocco, Colin had correctly confined his bathing to cold slime.

By the third week, the drilling and riding were being held in costume. The actors and extras had to adapt to the pinching of a pre-cast breastplate in the desert heat, fitted after sessions with their (often female) make-up teams. 'Antigonus' was waiting excitedly for his wounded 'one-eye': "it was supposed to happen today, but the packet containing it

118

was taken off the plane with an extra half a ton of armour and arrows and boots". As the baggage multiplied and the infantry units built up to a strength of nearly a thousand, the pressures multiplied on Dale Dye. It was relatively easy to make the men drill tightly into a 'locked shield' formation and reduce the space between each of them to about a yard. It was harder for them to advance quickly while holding the long sarissas which had arrived, with butt spikes, from Richard Hooper and the armoury division. The ancient texts even describe the sarissa-bearing line as moving fast or 'at a run': after experiment, Dale Dye's answer was typically forthright. "They didn't: the historians are lying". Manoeuvring sideways to change direction, proved even more difficult: the Captain had decided on the method of oblique marching, whereby the right-hand ranks led forwards and at an angle.

The cavalry too were practising with their long, thick lances, tipped with rubber points, and learning to balance them in the right hand. The campers increasingly came out into human contact, where the meals, women and cigarettes in the supporting trailers became dreadfully tempting. With Moroccan help, Ian had already smuggled in a few cans of Coca Cola and secretly shared them with Colin round the fire. He had even managed to smuggle in some eggs and cook them for egg-sandwiches in what seemed like a lifetime over the fading embers. By "Day 15, I am thoroughly fed up with this place now as are most of the other people here. Everyone is getting really short with each other…". Would Jared (Hephaestion) come to blows with Gary (Cleitus)? Had Johnny (Cassander) got a really bad ulcer? People were having the oddest dreams: Ian kept dreaming he was walking down the path outside his home in Belfast and telling a lady, "I'll see you later in the desert". Others simply fainted in the daytime. Even Dale Dye's key officer, the trusted Billy Budd, passed out in the sun and had to be taken to hospital. Billy was supposed to be the toughest of the tough.

The contrast between the food outside the camp and the food inside it was becoming acute. By Day 16, dinner failed to appear altogether in boot-camp after an afternoon of normal life. "Morning, September 18: have Colin and Rosario got something going together? Was I hallucinating with my one good eye, but weren't they snogging the faces off each other in make-up this morning? If so, good on them: whoever they were, they seem to be having a little fun…". Rumours started to spread that Captain Dye's years of military service had only been spent in the cooking-corps. Back in boot-camp, nonetheless, dinner was quick to run out again. Ian Beattie was now acclimatised to his patched-out eye and it was time for the ordeal to stop. The phalanx drilling was far from perfect after only two weeks of the manoeuvres which Philip had practised for twenty years. But the actors really knew each other's strengths, weaknesses and potential antagonisms. Out of hardship, a rare team spirit had formed around Colin. As Leonnatus (Garrett Lombard) remembered, Peter Ustinov once said of his military service that he "hated every moment, but would not have missed it for the world". No sooner was boot camp over than the actors began to be fiercely proud of it. Whatever Oliver's schedule might throw at them next, it would never be worse than Dale Dye's idea of a Macedonian lunch.

Tough wrestling trainer Leonidas (Brian Blessed) looks on at the boys in the Pella gymnasium.

13. Dressing Up

In boot-camp the male stars could wear their khaki underpants, or nothing at all, but out on the screen everyone's costume would be critical. The script brought Alexander into contact with a wide range of foreign cultures, Babylonian, Persian and Indian. Each one would have to be separately dressed. Oliver also had a clear vision of the styles and colours of each section in his six-part web of a story. Each of them must be separately colour-coded to support the audience's sense of changing time and space. Clothing, he also knew, had a special significance in Alexander's history. After capturing the dead Persian king, Alexander changed his 'image' and openly presented himself as Darius's respectful heir, the new King of Asia. A Macedonian king dressed quite simply, perhaps putting on a gold and purple cloak when not in battle, but (as far as we know) he never wore a jewelled crown. A Persian king wore a special upright headdress, the 'tiara' (whose nature is still disputed): some of the sculptures show him wearing a fluted sort of crown: like other courtiers, he wore that most un-Greek item, trousers. As the film shows, Alexander changes his costumes and looks much more exotic after capturing Darius' corpse. In antiquity his historians argued about the effect of this new dress: was he becoming a barbarian tyrant, not a king? Did he even dare to wear trousers, a tiara and an oriental cape? Oliver has described luxury as 'even more corrupting than battle', and Roman historians took a similar view, claiming that Alexander's costume was the proof that he was corrupted and was changing for the worse.

In fact, Alexander never wore trousers as a regular part of his public dress. He never wore a crown-tiara and he avoided fancy capes, high heeled shoes and Persian cosmetics. In the film, he wears the 'Persian' trousers for his wedding-ceremony to Roxane in his most 'Persia-friendly' moment and also for relaxed scenes in his tent between the Balkh fort and India. But in public, his main change as King of Asia was simply to wear a purple under-tunic with a white stripe and a coloured belt. This costume is historically well attested and refutes the more extreme views which were put about by his later ignorant critics: Alexander did not 'go oriental' to the same degree as Lawrence of Arabia. Filming, however, forced a historian like myself to realise that the ancient dispute over 'trousers' and 'decadence' addressed only one aspect of Alexander's wardrobe. It was chilly enough for the actors in our Balkh fort or when bare-legged in winter at Pinewood's Babylon, but for Alexander it was utterly freezing in the Eastern winters and mountains. He must have worn much more than the costumes about which the ancient sources disputed. While crossing the snowy Hindu Kush, Colin therefore wears furs. As a keen hunter of wild animals, Alexander surely did the same, although none of his critics discusses the warmer layers of his dress.

Back in Babylon, near the end of his short life, he was then said by his enemies to have been dressing up as one of the Greek gods or even as a goddess (Artemis). Again, there was surely slander and exaggeration here to please a hostile readership in Greece: perhaps he was wearing attributes of a particular god's image to express his special relationship with him or to conduct a sacrifice or an offering. In contemporary art, therefore, we find Alexander, wearing a lion's head helmet like the hero Heracles: again, the film picked up the hint and costumed Colin in one. At the final drinking party in Babylon, ivy-wreaths of the god Dionysus and a hat with feather-wings (the god Hermes's style) were worn by the guests as playful allusions to this divine world. By then, Alexander was receiving "honours equal to those of the gods" and a divine cult in some of his subject Greek cities. The dress at the party-scene makes the point.

In the Persian King's palaces, Alexander also captured a vast precious store of fine dresses and purple-dyed clothing. They were an important and often forgotten asset which royalty had amassed, as modern princesses still do. It was a shame that he never passed it all on to Hollywood. Instead, research began in early June at Pinewood on the bewildering array of costumes which would be needed on screen within only three months. Oliver then changed the team and on the advice of producer Iain Smith, appointed the highly-regarded Jenny Beavan to take over the entire responsibility. Now in her mid-career, Jenny had moved from theatre and opera to win an Oscar for the costuming of 'Room With a View' and eight other Oscar nominations, including one for 'Gosford Park'. She had just finished work on 'Byron' for the BBC and a theatre-play with Judi Dench and Maggie Smith at London's National. The invitation to design Alexander was a challenge on a huge and irresistible scale.

For Gaugamela alone, more than fifteen hundred costumes in at least twenty styles were needed. In scenes like Philip's murder or the entry into Babylon, the spectators would run to many hundreds and their costumes must vary with each person's age, sex and class. Jenny was able to call on her recent experience with the massive job of costuming the film 'Anna and the King'. There would be an Oriental dimension in 'Alexander' too, and the contacts she had made for 'Anna' in the Far East would be very useful. When faced with big projects, she tries to break them down into bits and take them one by one, in what she calls 'bite-sized chunks'. So she read the script, six times in all, noting the places where clear clues to costume were already given in Oliver's directions. She also bought the simple illustrated handbooks of Macedonian and other ancient soldiers, which are published in England as the 'Osprey' series for £6.99 each. The costume budget would have to be vastly bigger: it eventually reached £5 million.

Jenny's aim is always to "create the Director's vision". But what exactly did this one want? He was insisting on a separate colour range for each separate setting in his story because this 'coding' would intensify its moves to and fro. Alexandria, the future, was to be white, matching Jan Roelfs's visionary whites and greys: Babylon, to Oliver's eye, must be strong red, gold and blue. But what about the battle of Gaugamela with its multi-ethnic Persian army? The Macedonian soldiers were fixed by historians' reconstructed pictures, but what about Colin himself? What, too, about the fort in Bactria, exotic India and all the while, the important 'parallel stories' which are running on in the Macedon of Alexander's youth?

For India, there was not much colour-guidance in such ancient sources of the period as I could send her: white cotton, hair gathered up in a top knot, sunshades, jewellery and earrings seemed to be the most important items. The Babylon of Alexander's day is equally uncertain, as most of our evidence belongs many centuries earlier. At Pinewood, Oliver referred his team to film-evidence instead. For Babylon, he showed them D.W. Griffiths's Intolerance, made in 1917. A famous scholar of the time had hailed the "Babylonian scenes as magnificent, as well as true to facts," and it is still a classic. For India, he showed the Indian 'Bollywood' epic from the 1990's about their king Asoka who had lived some 50 years after Alexander. For the Macedon scenes, he was insisting on 'harsh whites and primary colours', but Jenny is not someone who goes often to the cinema and could not visualise what he wanted. Oliver explained by showing her the springboard of his thinking here, Jean Luc Godard's Le Mépris (Mistrust). Look carefully, he told her, at the image of a girl in an orange sweater against a blue door. By watching the film, she understood that costumes of monochromes (mainly using white) should be matched with 'individual colour-patches'. The striking colour of the most intense Macedonian scenes thus emerged by mutual agreement: white was to predominate, whites for Philip and almost all the guests at the wedding and murder scenes, but red for Philip's bodyguards and red to pick out Olympias (Angelina) with her scorn for the occasion and her possible role in Philip's death. The one ancient description of the theatre scene says that Philip did indeed wear white. Earlier, at Philip's wedding-party, the contrary colour would be yellow, yellow for the hateful Attalus and for Philip's other mistresses (he had seven women, most of them with children, by that time). To Jenny, yellow would convey a 'rather shifty' message, while the dominant whites as a contrast would enhance the intensity of Alexander's memories of childhood.

A use of cotton-white in India would not now be distinct enough and so Jenny started to range more widely. The film of Asoka helped her thinking on shapes, but what she called the "sherbet colours" emerged in discussion. Director of photography Rodrigo Prieto urged a dominant use of greens and oranges, colours which would stand up well to the film-processing which he was planning to use for the Indian outdoor scenes. Pinks came in too, and as Indian costume in the 320's BC is so little known, colouring from later Mogul India would reinforce the audience's sense of where the actors were supposed to be. The outstanding problem was still Bactria: what should be the dominant colours for Roxane's wedding and for the scenes in her father's fortress? Oliver then came up with an article from the National Geographic magazine which showed horsemen in modern Afghanistan and adjacent Central Asia wearing robes of indigo, faded red and brown. So was born the superb combination of muted reds, bronzes and dark purple-blue worn by Roxane's home countrymen.

Oliver, gaining confidence, was now teasing his new Costume Director. He kept telling her that she would probably try to make it all look 'Merchant Ivory': Jenny had already worked on twelve Merchant Ivory films. If not, would she not make it all 'horribly BBC'? The period dramas on British television tend to look absurdly clean and fresh, with newly-laundered aprons and soldiers in shining uniform. Oliver wanted coded colours, but not a ridiculous cleanness: in all his war-films, the battles are dirty and stressful and rooted in reality. Jenny understood, but replied in kind. "And I suppose you want it to look like some bad 1950's Hollywood big movie". "But I like bad Hollywood big movies of the 1950's," Oliver countered.

In all her work on 'historical' drama, Jenny's wish is to be "as historically accurate as possible: I try to know the truth, and then I deviate where necessary". Before Jenny took over, costume-research had consulted such books as Thomas Hope's 'Costume of the Ancients', published in 1809. Its image of Greek dress was badly distorted by the taste of its own era and it would have given the film a stiff, inauthentic look, as it had already given other film epics which had used it. Instead, Jenny set to work with Lloyd Llewellyn-Jones, the expert whom I had introduced to the Production team at the Oxford meeting. Lloyd fed Jenny's interest in the historic clothing which is shown on actual Greek vase-paintings, terracottas and stone sculptures. One challenge was to transfer the fashions shown in two dimensions in Greek vase paintings into three dimensions for actual wearers. Another was to work out how the sculptured costumes were really made and allowed to hang on a body. Jenny worked from books, from visits to the British museum, from the set designer's archives and from the ancient pictorial sources which Lloyd kept bringing over to Pinewood. Her team rose to the challenge and a team led by costume designer Stephen Miles, cutter Frances Hill and co-ordinator Dulcie Scott ran off Greek tunics, mantles (himatia), Persian capes and Macedonian cavalry cloaks (chlamydes) as prototypes. They were then dressed and pinned onto dummies in order to find out how best they would hang and how they should be fitted. Lloyd felt he was engaged in the research team of a lifetime. He, Jenny, and cutter Jane Law worked out for the first time exactly how a Persian noble's cape was fitted: it went over a noble's head, like a poncho, as a single sheet with a hole in it and it was then settled down by turning the arms "in a sort of swimming motion". The heavy, many-layered 'look' suited a Persian nobleman's dignified life-style. By contrast, a Greek could wear his tunic and cloak with 'negligent elegance', a more 'cool' style with so much more freedom of movement.

Usually, male actors will wear more or less anything: as Philip, Val Kilmer would even have to be seen in black, with furs, but he threw himself wholeheartedly into his 'animal' look. For Philip and Alexander, Jenny jumped at the chance to imitate clothing which had been discovered as recently as 1977 in the royal double tomb, surely Philip's own, at the ancient Macedonian capital of Vergina. Val Kilmer thus went on set archaeologically up-to-date as Philip in Philip's newly found iron-and-gold breastplate. Colin, too, received a look based on the new finds. Weeks of work by textile artist Sarah Shepherd imitated the acanthus-leaves and scrolls in the fabulous surviving fragments of the Macedonian royal robe which had been found in a lady's tomb-chamber, surely Philip's last controversial wife,

Ptolemy (Elliot Cowan) and Alexander (Colin Farrell) look out from the Hindu Kush on the way to India.

A joyful Alexander (Colin Farrell) with Ptolemy (Elliot Cowan) proposes a toast at his wedding in Bactria.

Olympias (Angelina Jolie) looks on coolly at the fateful scenes in Aigai's theatre while Hephaestion, Ptolemy, Parmenion and Antigonus applaud to her left.

A disapproving Roxane (Rosario Dawson) looks on at Bagoas's dancing during the Indian feast.

the young Eurydice. Its style was surely fit for princes too, and so it was adopted for Colin's royal cloak, a brilliant tribute to the most amazing find in recent Greek archaeology.

Oliver, too, caught the excitement, but remained anxious about the best type of purple to use in the nobles' cloaks. Lloyd explained how the ancients used a special dye, extracted from the shells of special molluscs in the seas off parts of Greece and the Levant. "Can we get these molluscs quickly?" Oliver alarmed the production team by exclaiming: in fact, the colour is now replicated artificially. The more difficult problem was the style of female dress.

In Macedonia, should the women wear veils? The Greek language has several words for 'veil' or 'covering' which are used in connection with women, whether Pandora, the mythical first woman, or others in Alexander's day. We also have many painted terracotta Greek figurines of women, some of which have been found in graves during Alexander's lifetime, especially at Athens and in Thebes, the city which he destroyed. These 'Tanagrans' show young women who often have their hands covered or hold prominent fans or have their faces almost totally veiled. However, experts think that many are courtesans and the heavily-veiled ones are dancers. Would women in Macedon also appear in public with a thin veil or at least with a cloak over their lower face? It would be a shame not to see Angelina's beauty, but might she be veiled outdoors, at least at the horse market? On painted Greek vases, however, women's faces are not usually veiled: Oliver correctly concluded that for Greek women, including Olympias, veils should not be worn.

For the Bactrian princesses, it was another matter. Lloyd knew two seal-rings from the Persian Empire which showed the drapes, veils and costumes of what appear to be ladies at the Persian court. The film's costumes were developed from these seal images, with the knowledge that Persian costumes tended to be heavy, in layers. When in doubt, clues were found in female costumes used later in eastern Iran. As a result, Roxane (Rosario) appears heavily veiled, at least initially: her red brocade costume is much more substantial than anything worn by Olympias; her wedding-dress is also red, red being a widespread 'wedding colour' in antiquity. By now Jenny was hunting out heavy Oriental fabrics for this style of dress: when Lloyd left on holiday for Istanbul, she encouraged him to buy any heavy silver jewellery and wedding-headdresses of the types made for Turkomen brides in Central Asia. He returned with a batch from Istanbul's Grand Bazaar, all of which were used in the dancing scenes. For the eunuch Bagoas (Francisco), there were hints in the carvings of beardless young men which have been found at the Persian palace of Persepolis. They implied that these beardless eunuchs wore an ornamental livery, and so Bagoas's court-dress became a uniform with red and gold circles.

On most movies, the crowd costumes and many of the principals' outfits are simply hired from costume-agencies. 'Alexander's' novelty, its colour-coding and its strong roots in history made hiring impossible. Jenny and the team thus found themselves in the rare position of having to buy raw fabrics and make them into individual costumes. Here they were at risk to the two constant enemies: time and money. There were only three months left for clothing the entire Persian army and it was a big crisis for the costume department when the film's financing went on hold in July and early August. If the entire wardrobe was to be bought afresh, suppliers would insist on a big down-payment. The ordering of hundreds of pairs of specially made cavalry boots becomes impossible if no money can be paid in advance.

Once again, Intermedia and Moritz Borman risked their necks, knowing that the schedule was genuinely at stake: if there were no boots and no uniforms, there would be no Gaugamela. Fortunately, there was also a coup by the buyers. The forthcoming 'Troy' film and the previous 'Alexander' projects had at least helped to gear up suppliers to the needs of Greek epics: Colin's robes for the Indian feast were made from striped materials originally commissioned for 'Troy'. But there were still problems. The first pricings for the Persian army clothes, if printed in Morocco, came out impossibly high. In Morocco, the affordable fabrics tended to be viscose which was too light and would never hang well. 'Fabric-scouts', therefore, went out to scour sources in Thailand, India and Pakistan. Crucially, co-producer Iain Smith then intervened and with costume buyer Ros Ward bought lorry-loads of printed and embroidered fabrics from the abandoned 'Alexander' series of HBO. This buy made the mass-costuming possible and saved the schedule.

Jenny also had her experts on the markets abroad. The Pinewood team staff found fast-moving factories in India, including the experienced 'Launch Early', based in Delhi. In England, orders were placed with teams in Biggleswade and the Greek-run firm of Costas, the noted theatrical experts. Stephen Miles's motto became "One size fits a lot", as the prototypes for crowd and army costumes went quickly off from himself and Dulcie Scott to Morocco and India. Indian suppliers happened to have the right weave of loose cotton for the Macedonian soldiers' cloaks, essential if they were to hang well and to stand up to heat, dirt and simulated blood. Above all, Anna Kot made crucial progress in Thailand. From her work on 'Anna and the King', Jenny had teamed up with Paothong Thongchua, a highly respected historian of textiles and costume, now in his late forties, who had family links with the Thai royal house and a job as Faculty Dean in Bangkok University. The 'sherbet colours', the heavier Bactrian cloth and some of the embroidered fabrics became accessible at short notice with 'Pan's' expert help.

Military helmets also found a quick, appropriate source. A few examples survive of real Macedonian cavalry helmets, which are fluted at their edges: one specimen was even recovered in 1854 from the Tigris river in modern Iraq where a Macedonian might have thrown it. Infantry helmets of a pointed 'Phrygian' style survive too, and we have a recently-found example from Ioannina, in Olympias' home-kingdom. Remarkably, we know how the ancients mass-produced them: from Egypt we have a surviving sculpted stone mould onto which the metal plates of each helmet would have been hammered by armourers. The 'Alexander' team knocked up metal prototypes, but sent them to various proven producers, Dave Cubbage and others up in Shropshire or FBFX in Feltham, London, who ran off hundreds of copies, but nowadays in polyurethane.

The main unsolved problems were the costumes for the Persian king's infantry. The decision to include Ethiopians in the Persian army gave a suitable 'multi-national' look, as did a unit of camels: both were accessible to the Persian Kings, who used them in war, although only the camels are attested at Gaugamela. The spotted leopard skins of the

Ethiopians could be designed and run up from artificial fabric without too much difficulty. The Persians' famous Immortals, however, are known for wearing golden robes with sumptuous patterning. The British Museum and the Louvre now hold the 'prototypes', the figures on glazed tiles which were excavated in the Persian palaces, but how could they be transferred to a fabric? First thoughts had been to print the entire pattern as a special run in Morocco, but the cost turned out to be prohibitive. Jenny's eye was then caught by some of the horse-blankets for the Persian nobles which were being decorated with applied, embroidered panels. Why not catch the Immortals' range of colours more cheaply by embroidering panels of colour and braid onto a basic brown-gold background? But were these elaborate costumes only the Immortal Guards' ceremonial palace-dress? Here, the 'Alexander Mosaic' filled in the picture, as the costumes of its Persians in battle are also very showy, with mixed colours. So, the stunning costumes of the Persians' archers and spearmen were developed for the film's front ranks. With the red and indigo Bactrians (wearing an imaginative plate of armour on their backs) they made even me suspend my Macedonian loyalties and feel just a twinge of sadness that their army, so handsome, could not win. In 1917, the film 'Intolerance' inspired American 'Back to Babylon' dresses: will 'Alexander' promote a 'Back to Bactria' look?

In a film there are no costume parades before dress-rehearsals. Instead, prototypes and drawings went off for Oliver's and Intermedia's approval. The trouble was that the Immortals looked potentially so handsome that Oliver now wanted to increase their numbers: would enough fabric exist? Extra panels of green and blue would also be needed to ensure that the costumes' old gold colouring would stand out in very strong desert sunlight. For the Indian battle, the cameramen were to use a 'bleached by-pass technique' which would heighten whites and make them look much too strong. Jenny's team would have to dye down the Indians' white cottons to a shade of fawn to survive this technical decision. From 'Anna and the King's' location in Malaysia, she also knew that unless she started with strong clear tones, the Eastern sunlight would kill their impact. The Macedonians, at least, were fixed in their off-white cloaks and body armour, but would the cotton-weave really stand up to a cavalry charge and to wounds and washing?

In August, a wardrobe team for work on location was finally assembled. There was an obvious choice for the supervision of each day's dressing: the redoubtable Rosemary Burrows who brings years of experience to the necessary calculations. Rosemary's definition of her role was typically direct: "Tents, Frocks and Toilets". In Morocco and Thailand, she would have to oversee the dressing of two entire armies each morning and then their undressing and their costumes' repair and cleaning each evening. To the producers' alarm, she insisted on a gigantic area of tenting, masses of clothes-hangers and a calculated back-up, including mobile toilets. But she was right, and fortunately they trusted her: those of us who saw the queues of multi-ethnic troops lining up at 5:30 am for their cloaks, breastplates and underpants could only bless her for her calculation of the necessary changing-space, correct to the last spare metre.

The stars, meanwhile, had been preceded by measurements and body-casts, though Colin's had been taken somewhat at an angle as it was cast on the day of his birthday celebration. Years of practice have taught Jenny to keep underpants in stock, as so many of the male film stars do not arrive wearing them. She is also well used to stars' uncertainties about the costumes put before them. However, Colin entered into the spirit of it all, trying on everything offered and showing it off to an enthusiastic Claudine who was also there for the fun. Wearing his lion-helmet or a stray breastplate, he would retire outside the Zoom building at Pinewood for the occasional cigarette, surprising passers-by with his unselfconscious style in Macedonian armour and jeans.

Would Roxane accept the heavy-layered Bactrian costume and a face-veil which began by obscuring her? Fortunately, Rosario threw herself into it too, playing with whatever was offered and saying about the veil what nobody else believed, that she was "better out of sight". In Babylon, her dress then shows her married and pregnant, but she played with the pregnancy padding and amused the team by simulating labour-pains. For Angelina, there was still an unsolved choice: should she follow the other Macedonian ladies and wear the historical Greek style of a cloak and an under tunic or should she go for a style as a queen which was more distinct? Her part has many emotional moments, and it would be hard to move freely in a historically-correct dress pinned on either shoulder and on the arms as far as the elbows and then left to fall in pleats from a loose belt about the waist. The alternative was to adopt a dress with a 'bias' cut, sloping off one shoulder and leaving the other shoulder bare, while the waist was gathered to give a more fixed shape. After discussion and comparison, she, Oliver and the team opted for the second solution, knowing that it was not historically attested for a Greek lady. But Olympias was a queen and a forceful character: who could say what might not have been the preferred item in her wardrobe? The choice underlines her strong character.

In action, Colin's helmet and breastplate would have to have a strong character too. There is one ancient text about his armour at Gaugamela, but it has none of the detail of the best-known ancient representation of him, again in the famous 'Alexander Mosaic'. Although it probably does not show the Gaugamela battle, it has much the best surviving depiction of his breastplate, decorated with the head of the stony gorgon Medusa. So, Jenny and the armourers copied it. It also shows Alexander going in to fight bare-headed, like a bold sportsman without a helmet, but the picture is only symbolic here, and coin images and texts show that on other occasions he wore a helmet with two upright plumes. From a surviving ancient helmet we can even see how such plumes were fixed into tubular holes. So, Alexander acquired a lion's head helmet, like the helmet which he wears in an ancient sculpted panel of himself in action. Out of it, as visual markers, flared the two plumes which the film deploys at Gaugamela, fixed in the ancient manner. His supporting cavalrymen, meanwhile, had a choice: either a silvered helmet with a single off-white crest, or a fluted silver helmet with a golden wreath attached to it. The wreathed style, too, was copied exactly from the 'Alexander Mosaic'. There, a warrior is set beside the charging Alexander and Bucephalas. His spear is following Alexander's, but historians still cannot identify this companion in the wreathed helmet. Among all the lorry-loads of costumes, I had the chance, for a few days, to solve the question by playing his part myself.

Opposite page: Robin Lane Fox on Gladiator leads the charge at Gaugamela.

14. AT THE CHARGE

Clothed and trained, the cast was ready to go out on set from September 19th onwards. Into the Moroccan desert went a crew of anything from make-up artists and animal handlers to cooks, armourers and experts in 'special effects'. The production team of five hundred people travelled like Darius's Persian army rather than Alexander's lean, hardened troops. Transport was in the hands of a proven Moroccan team, managed by Hicham Regragui: there was no point in economising on the type of vehicle, as a single break-down would immobilize an entire scene. Between four locations in Morocco, over nearly two months, the cost of transporting this travelling circus was more than 1.3 million dollars, paid directly into the Moroccan economy. From a distance, the outdoor locations looked like a cross between a race-meeting and a caravan-site. In 'Natural Born Killers' (1994), being on location with Oliver was described as "purgatory on a per diem". On Alexander, there were tough moments of hell, but the impression was one which nobody, not even a historian, would forget.

As a serving cavalryman, I can best evoke the film's two contrasting battles, Gaugamela in Morocco and 'India' in Thailand. On set, the crew's life is guided by daily Call Sheets, drawn up on the previous evening with the approval of Oliver, the Assistant Directors and Heads of Department. On both locations, the day was planned to begin extremely early. In Morocco, after weather-forecasts and a list of the three or four scenes to be filmed, Call Sheets would specify: "pick up Jared Leto and Jonathan Rhys Meyers at 6:15 am and convey to Location Base – battlefield": by 6:45am, Colin would be on the road too. The journey from our Marrakesh hotels to the desert-set was a drive of about forty minutes, but in Thailand the commute from the Bangkok traffic-jams to the 'jungle' was up to 1¾ hours, even at the hurtling speed of our keen Thai drivers. In Bangkok the order would be to "pick up Neil Jackson and Ian Beattie at 5:45 am and convey to Location Base", with Colin setting out by 6am. Even those stars, like Colin, who seldom slept for as much as three hours were always punctual, changing in their trailers with their hairdresser and costume specialist. Within days, Colin had his uniform down to a fine art, taking twenty minutes, two cigarettes and a coffee to put it all on, even while the helmet was of heavy metal. No schedule on location was kept waiting by unpunctual actors.

At the other end, the working day ended outdoors at 6 pm with a final shot, the 'wrap shot'. But the timing might slip on, and in neither place were we back from the vans until nearly 8pm. Fresh from my university life, I found myself living two academic working days in the space of one. Unlike most of the stars, I was too flattened to spend a further hour 'de-stressing' at night in the hotel gym. There was only one familiar landmark: the food. Like Oxford colleges, film-sets provide their staff with a free, hot breakfast and a choice of free lunches. Even in the desert heat of Gaugamela, a two-course lunch and lunch-hour were sacrosanct, although the site was miles from running water or a town. Trucks brought in curry or stew for fifteen hundred: film-food is better than a university lunch.

In the pale early morning light, nearly a thousand warriors would pour into Rosemary Burrows's big clothing tents at location-base and fill them with a male, multilingual babble. The previous day's cotton cloaks all had to be relocated and fitted with shoulder-clasps; the moulded breastplates went on with leather straps and buckles; underneath, we wore only tan-coloured knickers, lace-up boots and a secret unknown to Aristotle, elasticated socks. From the tent gangways, stars and Europeans then headed for the make-up teams to be dabbed with bronzing lotion and cosmetics. On big cavalry-days, I would be made up with a lurid arm-wound of acrylic paint, applied by Dave, a former make-up artist on British TV's serial 'Brookside'. On good mornings, the beauticians would even insist that I needed 'ageing'.

The clothing and make-up sectors were the concealed heart of the entire day's system. In Morocco, after our dressing, scores of hairdressers might find themselves sticking bits of black felt onto plastic bowls, their dummy-faces, and peeling them off when they had made a complete beard. Five hundred or so of these beards might be needed for Persian and Bactrian soldiers on any one day. The beauticians, meanwhile, were under orders to shave the leg-hair off every cavalryman. The king of Morocco had commanded that all genuine taxi-drivers in the country should grow moustaches. Oliver had decreed that all horse-riders should be shaved.

After make up we were crammed by the dozen into trucks among the big lorries for the day's quota of cavalry-horses. The entire convoy was like an English early-morning fox-hunt, with the desert location as the 'meet'. Between wake-up calls and the first take of the day, it was inevitable that four hours would pass by, because some 1250 actors had to be armed and correctly stationed. In Morocco, the forces were usually divided into two units, the cavalry under Oliver's direction, and the infantry, a mile away, under the direction of Dale Dye, dressed in his khaki shorts and a shirt with a tough Latin motto about Death. On both sets, orders would be relayed in English, then French and Arabic for the Moroccan soldiers' benefit. Alexander's armies in India had faced similar problems with interpreters, as tens of thousands of Indians joined the army in order to attack their bothersome fellow-Indians.

On First Unit, Oliver would be established early by the Director's Tent in the red or blue sports shirts which were his wardrobe. Script-writing he regards as a form of turning inwards, whereas direction on set is one of turning outwards. Inside, a camera-monitor would forewarn him of each proposed angle and show him every action-shot. Beside him stood a core-staff, ranging from script supervisor Sue Field to his assistant directors and any Heads of Department whom he might need. Between all the key personnel, communication was by mobile phones, whether for camera-angles, the placing of dummy dead bodies or for special effects as listed on the day's Call Sheet: "As per Trevor Wood, incense smoke thickens the air, campfires, flaming torches, smoke, swords being sharpened. As per John Scheele, Eclipse of moon". Throughout, by Oliver's side, was the man most concerned to see each of his wishes realised: first 'A.D.' Simon Warnock, armed with a loud hailer. Simon's infinite patience and good humour were crucial to the set's functioning and from him, 'no secrets were hid' on good days or bad. While everyone was taking up their position and while the camera on its truck and crane was moving to the right place, second assistant director Michael Stevenson would firmly move extras out of the light and keep up morale with his own enthusiasm and example. One of cinema's most respected figures, Michael found the heat no problem. Earlier in life he had served under canvas for ten weeks in the desert with David Lean's 'Lawrence of Arabia'. His personal touch and his integrity made us all try not to let him down.

Arriving for cavalry service from Oxford's libraries, I was treated to grim reports by the costume teams in the hotel bar in Marrakesh. I must be mad; three Moroccans had fallen off their horses on the first day and were in hospital; Cassander had already cut his mouth by pulling upwards on his horse's head. The welcome pack contained warnings from Cindy Irving that scorpions and snakes lived in the desert too, that sandals were banned and that day-temperatures were so high that water was a constant necessity.

In the hot morning light, we had our first apparent mirage: over the ridge came a cluster of three phalanx-syntagmata, armed with long sarissas and chanting Captain Dye's war-cry. In ancient Greek texts, the troops liked to 'alalalazein', shouting 'alalalai'. The Captain had tried it, but on the advice of Vangelis, the music composer, he had changed to the clearer chant of 'En-y-al-ios', a name of the Greek war-god. Should he have been in the vocative case (En-y-al-ie)? At the sight of so many sarissas and this fragment of phalanx-life, I could not help crying. Its eventual conqueror, the Roman Aemilius Paullus, used to say afterwards at dinner-parties in Rome that the phalanx was "the most terrifying thing" he had ever seen. Two thousand years later, its imitation had the same overpowering force: so this was what all the planning and paperwork had been about. But the key to Alexander's victory was the cavalry, and so they dominated the first two weeks of filming on First Unit.

Up on First Unit, I encountered Colin, galloping heroically down the ranks of the main phalanx and presenting arms on his black horse Bonze while he shouted uplifting lines to the microphone under his breastplate. It was almost unimaginable that he had only got on to this horse a month or so before. Telling me that "I'd given him eye-ache" by writing a long book, he left me to mount his horse-double, Bucephalas II, under the expert eye of horsemaster Ricardo Cruz Moral, while an amused group of make-up artists dabbed my shaved legs with brown cream. With Ricardo watching, it was for me to ride Talevan, the big black, in a controlled figure of eight and then repeat the move at the canter, to the barracking of members of the Moroccan Royal Squadron. Talevan obeyed the aids, and to acclimatize ourselves we set off for Dale Dye's Second Unit with star Spanish rider Luis Miguel beside us, urging us on to 'galopé'. On Second Unit, the guards saluted, Talevan neighed and we imitated Colin in a one-handed gallop down the front line of the phalanx while the rear ranks reclined in the hot sun. Such rest-periods were the recurrent blessing in their day.

Back on First Unit, Oliver welcomed us onto the set, warning me that I would now find out "what a slow, tedious business film-making is". Despite the protests of safety-assistants and horse-owners, he then packed me off, as he had promised so long before, to the front of the next cavalry-charge, the start of Alexander's famous turn from the right wing towards the centre. In the sand, we checked the correct manoeuvres, not a 'circle of 120 degrees', as the Call Sheet threatened, but as I explained, a straight swing to the left ("Turn left", Colin would shout in Irish-English) like a football wing-forward who was cutting in to goal. There was no Dale Dye and no high explosive, because the Captain was busy imploding on Second Unit. Until that point, the script-notes of Sue Field had recorded: "Oliver feels the cavalry lacked energy". A historian might hot them up.

On my wiry chestnut stallion, misnamed 'Gladiator', I galloped up to Colin's front line (courtesy of Oliver) and waited while cables, cameras and the crane prepared to follow us on a truck during our lance-held charge. At the real Gaugamela, the Persian Darius had levelled the ground for his horses and chariots and had fixed traps in the sand to impede Alexander's. At the film's Gaugamela, Oliver had ordered teams to clear stones off as much of the sand as possible: it was a hopeless task, and already two stunt-riders had been unseated by loose rocks. In our right hands we held the long wooden lances ten to twelve feet long with the rubber blades and balancing butt-spikes which Richard Hooper and his armourers had modelled on an ancient tomb-painting of a Macedonian horseman charging an Oriental footsoldier. There were no stirrups, and with a loose-fitting helmet and no buckle on the reins, I had Ricardo's unsure blessing. A mile-long race-track stretched ahead, flanked by Jared and Gary Stretch, who had practised for weeks, whereas I had not.

Acting, the stars now decided, was hell: hunting foxes sounded so much more enjoyable. Within hours, I had decided that six years on horseback, with no saddle, would have made Hephaestion's backside so hard and leathery that it was not in the least surprising if Alexander opted for a soft unmilitary Persian eunuch for a change: Bagoas took on a new appeal. "Tense up, gentlemen," Simon Warnock would call out on the loud hailer, "Cameras rolling… Charge". Away we surged, with Moroccans, skilled Spaniards and a hundred or so stallions raising billowing clouds of dust. "Turn left," the dominant Colin shouted, and most of us pulled leftwards, myself blessing Gladiator for his turning although my long cavalry lance by his right cheek was threatening to bash him in the eye. The race was multi-ethnic, the pace and energy far more intense than I expected, but within hours I found I had solved some academic puzzles. Yes, the 'on-horse-felt' cited by the Greek Xenophon was a padded horse-blanket, serving as a proto-saddle. No, charging Macedonian cavalrymen could not possibly have carried a shield on the left arm as well. Yes, their spears could be twelve feet long. Yes, they could charge an enemy, even without stirrups: between gallops, I practised charging at the willing Ibrahim and established, off camera, that a full-frontal strike into his chest was possible, even at the gallop. The

The Persian king Darius (Raz Degan) prepares for battle, surrounded by his courtiers.

Overview of the vast Persian army facing Alexander at Gaugamela.

Alexander (Colin Farrell) follows up at the charge after breaking through at Gaugamela.

The waiting Persian king Darius (Raz Degan) directs his opening moves at Gaugamela.

'Alexander Mosaic' is not lying when it shows Alexander executing such a blow. But the easiest method is to drive a lance, held horizontally in the right hand beyond Gladiator's neck, and ram it straight into an enemy's shoulder. Galloping past, you can then pull the spear after you, so long as it does not break. The notion that the long lances were thrown is completely false. They gave the charging Macedonians a longer, lethal 'reach' than their enemy's. On subsequent days, I tried them out on opposing Bactrians, most of them French-speakers, who rode off winged and unhappy, protesting that 'L'anglais est fou…'

For Colin's sake, I also discovered what Homer calls 'lyssa', the battle-fury which makes a hero go berserk. It is even better on four legs at a gallop. On the following Monday, while the stars wheeled left, it was given to me to lead the entire cavalry flat out down the desert 'gallop' ahead of us. "Serrez les rangs…" the orderlies would shout, "votre chef de charge est Professeur d'Oxford…" Word even spread that the last three would be castrated, together with their stallions. Flat out, and losing ground to the Berbers, I learned how little a cavalryman could have seen of an overall 'battle-plan'. Two ranks behind him, nobody could ever have seen what Alexander was doing. In the dust-clouds, only immediate neighbours are visible. Grounded historians have ignored its effect on the horses' lungs, eyes and stamina, as well as on the men. In the headlong pursuits, I understand why Alexander killed so many horses: they were short of water and clear air.

In the evenings, as the light went a magic mauve-purple, we would gallop out on a détour to descend from the foothills and take the last dastardly Bactrians by surprise. Down the rough hillside, Gladiator and the Moroccans would fight nobly for pre-eminence, flanked by a standard-bearer who suddenly surprised me in English. Never think you are the only one in life's odd settings: he identified himself as a security guard from London's store, Harrods, on secondment to Dale's Core. As we set an ambush with infantry hidden among our horses, English, again, emerged from the half-naked slingers around us in boxer-shorts. "Where are you from?" I asked them: "Jail", their leader Danny assured me. "We've just been let out of the nick in Norwich". Like the Duke of Wellington, Dale Dye had recruited the very 'scum of the earth'.

To a horseman's delight, each manoeuvre had to be repeated section by section in fragmented sequences. The entire crew's life becomes one of patient inertia for hours on end, punctuated suddenly by bursts of action which justify their day's endurance. Beauticians would spring forward, bronzing a historian or Gary Stretch, with one lady for the limbs, one (by demarcation) for the armour. And the scenes would be broken down into fractions: "Macedonian left. Parmenion wonders what magic this Boy King possesses." Then, "The Persian right flank: Cavalry smashes into the Macedonian infantry: the camera drops down through the dust." This one sequence might take five hours, with hand-held cameras filming boldly among our hooves. It might also bring the magic out of Oliver. "Adversity", he would often say, "is an ally…" or, "I hate the shot I have to do: what I want is the shot which I can improvise." In early October, a dust-storm broke and would have halted other Directors. In a flash, Oliver saw it could be the setting for his scene when Colin, after victory, is moved by the thousands lying dead on the battlefield. The dust and clouds lent force to a shot which stretched camera-skills to the full. Or, as

Parmenion held the left, Oliver would see a ravine to one side of the set and transfer the entire camera-team to exploit it, the setting for John Kavanagh's ringing call for help.

After hours of arrangement, the Persian chariots would charge and be 'mousetrapped', while spectacular camels would race down the right wing. At first, the Macedonian phalanx had lacked the final ounces of control and energy. After argument with the Captain, I had suggested that their sarissas should move up and down in unison, before battle-position was taken up. For hours, in hot sun, Dale Dye experimented and was hard pushed to achieve the result: perhaps, with hindsight, I had confused it with the sideways 'swishing' of sarissa-points with which the Macedonians did flatten fields of standing corn. But in the end they did it, a vivid prelude to battle. Why should Moroccan soldiers give every last drop of sweat to what was only a film? Pressure mounted on the Captain who was already stretched to the limit, and there were warning symptoms of a physical stroke. But he took only one day's rest and was back, in untamed form. All sympathies were rejected: it was nothing, Dale insisted, "only a brain-fart". And in response to the brain-fart, the phalanx improved.

As the stunt men prepared for their hand to hand fighting, it was time for a mere historian to return to University and teach others how Alexander won his victories. The hero, for me, was Gladiator and from Oxford, I decided to send him a box of apples and a pin-up photograph of a chestnut mare. But what was the French for a 'chestnut mare', so that his keeper could explain it to him? In the safety of the tea-room of my Oxford college, I asked a French-teaching colleague, as if it was only a routine question from one more day in the library. "I don't understand", she replied, "what is a 'chestnut mare'? Is it some sort of dessert?" It was actually a question from the desert. Between Oliver's battlefield and academia, there is a wonderful gap, and it would long sustain a cavalryman's smile.

Alexander (Colin Farrell) charges at Gaugamela with Robin Lane Fox on Gladiator in the dust to his left.

Opposite page: Robin Lane Fox awaits the next Indian elephant charge on set in Thailand.

15. WILD ON SET

The Morocco battle of Gaugamela was very closely based on the ancient historical accounts. The real dust-bound filming is the core and script-supervisor Sue Field's notes catch the hand-to-hand savagery of it. "Sept. 22: Handheld over Nearchus, with Persians to camera. Move in with him as he fights towards them with half-broken sarissa and then grabs a battleaxe from the Persians and continues to hack them down..." "Horses charge through frame. Perdiccas' helmet is pulled off by infantryman who bites his ear. Note: Oliver loved the cuts where Horse charged at Perd. And he ducked". After the live action, I drew a full battleplan, based on the ancient evidence, so that the scale could be increased by visual effects in post-production. We had to simplify some of the cavalry units on Alexander's right, and we left out the Greek mercenaries on the Persians' side, but we did add the second infantry formation behind Alexander's lines. We increased his numbers to 50,000 and the Persians to about 170,000 (Greek historians credited them with 'a million'). Dale Dye's plan had been different, but Oliver's Gaugamela is the most historically-based battle ever filmed from the ancient world.

In Thailand ('India'), the intention was different. To hold an audience, this second battle must have a very different flavour and would condense events in the interests of the script's plot. It would show the Macedonian army's stress and fear. They would hang back: the jungle forest would impede them; Alexander would gallop in alone against the enemy. He would be wounded and Bucephalas would die and then the Macedonians would surge in after him and take a terrible revenge. The colouring would be different and the type of camera-film would heighten it: even the Call Sheets expressed the change. "Make-up: as per Jeremy Woodhead, blood and gore. Special Effects, as per Trevor Wood: smoke, arrows in horses. Prosthetics, as per Steve Painter; Billy Budd crushed heads x3; dead horses". Above all, so did the enemy line-up. Through the jungle, to the sound of gongs and drums, would power a line of twenty four war-elephants, complete with howdahs and keepers (mahouts). "Elephant prosthetics: elephant tusks, legs, trunks, blood, knives..." The Call Sheet struck a new note of danger: "No cast should approach Elephants unless the Mahout is there. Never ever approach an Elephant from behind... The above note must be taken very seriously..." No Western film had ever set horses against elephants and nobody, before Oliver, had used so many elephants at once.

By this stage, animal-handling was not new for the 'Alexander' crew. Before filming in Morocco, Animal Coordinator Gill Raddings had searched the country for the script's other four-legged friends. In the Rabat zoo, she had found caged bears for Roxane's wedding and a caged lion, tiger and ostrich for the entry into Babylon's Gate. She had also found six suitable dogs at a local Rescue Centre. Mastiffs were not available in Morocco, so despite Jan Roelfs's notes from the Greek expert Konstantin Adamopoulos (www.moloss. com), Alexander's personal dog was a small greyhound, a Slugi. For sacrifice, Gill had even found two bulls. The more placid of the two was gratefully hired out by the owner of the fields on which the Horse Market scene was built. Nick-named 'Essa', he stayed calm among the crowds and statues in the theatre-scene of Philip's murder.

Animals are animals, and nothing is ever easy. For authenticity, Gill had searched in Morocco for the two-humped Bactrian camel which would be right for scenes in Bactria. She found two, on an animal farm, but before the crew arrived, one had died of old age and the other was looking rickety, so she had to use local camels instead. At the Babylonian Gate, Oliver was determined that a zebra should be led, without a cage. Wild zebras could not be trusted, so Gill took a white mule and painted it with stripes, using black vegetable-dye. Onlookers also had to hold peacocks, but in October peacocks have lost their tail feathers: the special effects team made up mock tails from bought-in feather-bunches. There were also transport and conduct problems. In Morocco, Gill found, carts and trailers do not have ramps, so the animals had to jump into them off roadside banks. On set, during slow set-up scenes, the local herdsmen misunderstood and sometimes started driving their sheep and goats home. Meanwhile, zoo-animals who arrived in cages had to be transferred into cages on set, a very delicate task in the sheer, confined setting of Roxane's fortress. Above all, the bulls had to be taught their part from scratch. In Morocco, bulls have short horns, or none, so Gill had to add false horns, knowing that bulls dislike having their horns touched. Trained handlers dressed in film-costume stood at the ready beside Essa or the more fiery Hero. As sacrificial animals they had to be sprinkled with water, but a dummy bull, of course, was then 'killed' and cut up in their place.

In Thailand, Gill had already been busy: she had recruited water buffaloes and thirteen monkeys from farms near Suritahni where they were employed to climb up trees and throw down the coconuts for their owners. In coaches, the monkey-team arrived to play with Hephaestion on camera. Not one single animal was ever sedated. Gill was not responsible for elephants, but after much scouting, the team was made up from the Ayutthaya Elephant Palace and Royal Krall, run by the masterly Sompast Meerpan. His elephants are well used to giving rides to tourists and performing individual tricks; how would they take to sarissas, cavalry and Oliver's 'New Wave' style of cameramen filming hand-held shots near their legs? It was no use sending Dale Dye to run a 'tusk camp': Dale could preside, but he had never faced an elephant, either. The fodder, at least, was no problem. A base camp was established within reach of a local Del Monte pineapple factory so that the leaves and tops of their pineapple crop could be brought in daily and added to the elephants' diet. Throughout, the expert vet Dr. Preetha Phuangkum joined Richard Lair, Foreign Relations Officer of the National Elephant Institute, in order to supervise training and conditions. Each elephant is devoted to its own special carer, or mahout, who would be dressed in Jenny's 'pearls and sherbet colours'. The mahout was

Alexander (Colin Farrell) charges alone through scattered Indian infantry to confront the leading war elephant.

Indian war elephants charge devastatingly through the Indian forest.

Alexander (Colin Farrell) rears up on Bucephalas in their fatal charge against the leading war elephant.

Alexander (Colin Farrell) gallops through the forest to unite with Hephaestion (Jared Leto), followed by Robin Lane Fox between the trees.

surrounded by three archers in the howdah and a team of five ('Zen's Ellie Guards') on the ground. One of the mahouts was a lady: each would sit well forward on their elephant, equipped with a pointed goad.

On the first day of drill, the elephants showed a marked dislike for sarissas held at the ready: they identified their blades with the points on their mahouts' goads. So the sarissas were replaced with sticks bearing red flags, and gradually, over two months, the elephants came to realise they were harmless. Tusks were also a problem. Not every elephant still had tusks and so prosthetic ones had to be fitted as 'tusk enlargements'. How ever would they react to battle-noise, as the infantry-fighting round them would be fierce? Each elephant had a strong personality, already trained by Sompast to individual specialities. One would stand up on its hind legs, another would hold its foot (so we trusted) above a person on the ground. Would they all break through a gap in the Macedonian lines while carrying archers in hand-made howdahs and wearing clothes of golden plate?

In January, I left my Oxford lecture-room where I had just described to a bemused audience the days immediately following Alexander's death: Craterus, Perdiccas, Ptolemy merged in my mind (and notes) with Rory, Neil and Elliot. From the lecture, it was a straight route by plane to Bangkok to meet my lecture-notes alive and hyper-active in the hotel bar. Even 'Alexander' appeared to have returned from the dead with a double dose of vodka. And on the next morning, at 5 am, it was off at once to the set.

I had expected a sweaty green jungle with trailing creepers and a tree-house for Tarzan. A vast, uncharted Botanical Garden was therefore something of a surprise. In the section for 'spurges', varieties of which had once blinded Alexander's horses, Rosemary Burrows had installed another huge male changing room. The Thai soldiers were being seconded to the set by regiment, and as truly professional troops they had already applauded Rosemary for her planning. As a tribute, they had even given her a military uniform. Beyond the breakfast tenting, the Co-ordinators' caravan looked out on a nursery-garden of trees in pots; then, the road wound up through rare botanical Cassinia trees growing in rock hard ground to the familiar battery of cameras and horseboxes and beyond, the Director's tent. Horseriding is always terrifying to anyone on foot, but this time, even the stars had been warning about the Thai cavalry horses. Cassander was already out of action; Ptolemy had grazed his legs and hands; one stunt man had hit a tree and broken a leg-bone; the horses and their hooded Thai riders were trained to ceremonial duty with the King, but not to a forest-battle with Oliver. Half-blinded in the sunlight, I was greeted by the Director while a furious infantry battle calmed down among the myrtaceous trees. Where had I been: it would be cavalry warfare all afternoon, and I was cast as 'Oliver's Fighter'?

While Colin led half of the cavalry up through the botanical trees, Jared (Hephaestion) was to lead me and the other half, flying past the cinnamon-trees and Rhododendron giganteum until the two units met at a bottle-neck, where Oliver had stationed Camera Number One. This time, our bodies were bloodied with a sugary crimson liquid which smelt like sour tomato sauce. Cavalry-lances were optional, as many would have been broken in the previous assault, but drawn scimitars were not. In view of the terrain we had a new support: stirrups, which would be erased in post-production. Like Alexander's cavalry we also had Oriental cavalry with us, mounted Thais who sang enchantingly.

At the head of a botanical avenue, Hephaestion mustered us horsemen while ably rebuking his frisky chestnut horse. Mine, a royal black stallion called Chalabi, was more interested in the branches of rare relations of the Breadfruit tree. In front of us, teams of Thai gardeners were digging big obstacles into our flight line, clumps of the pampas grass which I hate in gardens. Has any gardening journalist, my other day job, ever been asked to gallop and jump over grass mounds between ornamental botanical trees, while his film-King is thundering in from the right? "Call something, Jared", Oliver's voice came over the microphone. "I love you, Alexander", Jared shouted into the forest. Colin shouted back, "I'll see to you afterwards" (or words to that effect), and we all had such laughter that the shot had to be delayed. Eventually, we were off at a storming pace, Jared curbing the chestnut, myself spurring Chalabi. In five happy takes, we united five times over with Colin's forest detachment and lost three of the clumsier stunt-men as they pulled too hard on their bridles when the two units collided. We surged on together without them.

As night drew on, smoke-clouds began to rise from the 'special effects' behind the forest, while drums and cymbals sounded from the hillcrest, as they had once sounded to Alexander's men. It was time for our first charge within sight of the elephants who would emerge from Jan Roelfs's jungle. In Jan's research notes, a book on bamboo explained, "A bamboo stem does not stand alone as does a tree in a forest: each stem is merely part of a greater plant which is the clump or grove". The man-made jungle was still being watered by 25 Thai groundsmen, as the dry season was not letting up. Under their artificial rain, elephants prepared to storm through a planting which they found as tasteless as I found pampas-grass, and therefore would not eat.

Stunt-coordinators were certainly not willing to risk a historian in the first rank against elephants, but by the third take, a stunt man or two had crashed into well-spaced tree-trunks and nobody was noticing if a historical horseman joined the melée. We bounded like hounds through the botanical specimens, reached the hill-crest and verified everything which historians have written from ground-level about horses when pitted against elephants. Chalabi saved me a brush with a safety officer by freezing in his tracks at the first sight of a howdah, then shaking and bolting sideways. The horses, of course, had been shown the elephants for weeks already, but I no longer believe historians who write as if all the horses in Indian armies were somehow 'accustomed' to the tuskers. In his main elephant-battle, Alexander's cavalry went off on a wide detour to the left which has puzzled military historians and their neat tactical maps. I now understand why: they were riding wide to avoid the elephants, and like Chalabi, their horses bolted left-handed, the horse's preferred escape route.

The next days were to be tense, even for Oliver. On walking the jungle-site, he had remarked to Dale Dye how he felt the proposed position for the infantry was badly exposed from the rear: Dale respects Oliver's 'feel' for a scene, and he now realised that elephants could also be brought up to attack the phalanx from behind. While Rory and Ian Beattie tried to steady the front ranks, Dale, in combat trousers, urged them to face about, countermarch and simulate fear and chaos against the new threat to their rear.

Whether Macedonians actually counter-marched or not, it was a hallmark manoeuvre of the U.S. Marines, and the Captain was wearing their hat.

Frontally, elephants now had to charge the wavering phalanx and career through their parted ranks. Beside them, individual Shield Bearers and commanders would set about their 'Ellie Guards' and attack the clusters of Indian-Thai archers. One specialist elephant would even stand poised with a foot above the prostrate Billy Budd: it was the least of Billy's worries that he was having his teeth re-set by Bangkok's excellent dentists at the time. "Cameras rolling...", Simon Warnock would begin. "Elephants forward... part ranks... Filming..." and on foot, cameramen risked the fray for hand-held shots below the elephants' bellies. To steel himself, Rory McCann had been listening to his native Scottish bagpipes on tape. He was so primed for battle that he set out in earnest with a drawn sword against three Thai troopers from 'Zen's core'. For the next take, he was limited to listening to Beethoven.

Magically, the elephants followed the corridors which opened in the ranks, with the minimum of trumpeting and the maximum pleasure in their public's applause. Their mahouts' day had begun at 4 am, washing each beast, then arranging for the 300 litres of water which each one needs. But the first big hurdle was over. From behind the lines, we cavalrymen simulated panic and retreat: Colin galloped by to stiffen our nerves ("Why are you hanging back?") while cameras mounted on quad-bikes careered along a hastily-laid track and followed him past our faces. The Oxford cavalryman found it hard to hang back and nearly jumped the track to follow Colin to his doom.

Everyone knew the next day's shots were the testing ones. Colin had to ride big Bucephalas through hundreds of battling and clashing footsoldiers, avoid the tree trunks and rear the horse up on its back legs in front of the biggest of the war-elephants, 'Tusker Castle', complete with tusk-enlargements and long knives. As he reared, a concealed wire would pluck him off backwards for a soft landing, we hoped, into a prepared earth-pit. Some of the scene could be pre-filmed with Colin wielding his sword on a specially-made mechanical horse. But reality would be needed too. The Macedonian and 'Persian'-Thai cavalry would then surge in fury against the elephant-line, while Dale's Core, Oliver's old age pensioners and the mass of hot and demoralised infantry would engage yet again in close combat, clashing their swords on polyurethane shields. Colin could then be escorted out on the armoury-department's masterpiece, their copy of Homer's Shield of Achilles. Mercifully, a 'parallel-story' would flash before his wounded brain, transporting the action off to Essaoueira (Aigai) and the scenes around Philip's murder which were safely in the 'can' three months before.

On the first few takes, 'Bucephalas' refused at the clatter of battle. Despite his best efforts, Colin was unable to control the rearing horse. His riding double, Rowley Irlam, took over with the Spanish master-horseman Luis Miguel: the horse approached, but the problem then became the elephant. Elephants are reluctant to go up on their hind legs and expose their soft underbellies to an approaching animal, because they worry that it may be a predator. Bucephalas I (Bonze) had taken against the fighting; Bucephalas III (Ubode) was the worst rearer, but he agreed to go right up to the elephant with Rowley and even to make friends. After further false starts, briefly the two animals did it, rearing up simultaneously on their respective hind legs in a magnificent tableau of 'East' against 'West' before the valiant Rowley was pulled off into the earth-pit, unscathed from his adventures.

It was then for the cavalry to surge after a shocked Hephaestion and run the gauntlet of tusk and trunk among the trees. Without the Spanish stunt-stars, we would probably never have got within fifty yards of the starting point. In a rush, they careered right past the elephants, driving their horses through the parted ranks of a close-combating phalanx. Elephant charging is not recommended if you are without your usual spectacles: I drove black Chalabi almost within tusking distance before he spun left-handed and lost himself in the Captain's clusterf***. An elephant will charge in self-defence at up to 30 mph, but in thirty seconds I learned how to read the elephant-battles of Alexander's successors with new eyes. Their cavalry, too, refused to face elephants head on, even though they had been living among them for months. They left the attack to horse-archers at long range, except for those who had plainly read Oliver's Call Sheets and learned to attack an elephant-column in the rear, which "can frighten them", not least because elephants carry their testicles high up in their back quarters.

For Oliver, as usual, there was a reward to be found in what was unscripted: no sooner were the elephant scenes mastered than he returned to another historical event, a meeting between Alexander and some Indian wise men. Buddhism, in Thailand, was all around us: could we find a tree, put Indian wise men under it and give them a script? Could we run up a relief of Buddha showing the influence of Greek art, in case Ptolemy might comment on the famous birth of a 'Greco-Buddhist' style? In a hot, pacified Botanical Garden, why not? Jan Roelfs and I checked out tree-trunks; Jim Erickson even found the most authoritative volumes on Greco-Buddhist art, two British Museum books, in a Bangkok market. Props ran up a 'Gandhara' Greek-style Buddha in less than a week, while Rob recorded my suggestions for the wise men's dialogue and Ptolemy's comments on the results. Having made film-history on trunk and tusk, we were now making up possible film-scenes like a school-play.

In the end, Oliver delayed the 'wise men' until the final filming at Ubon Ratchathani. The 'Buddhist' comments had to be left out, but up there, they tell me, a fine replica of Buddha now nestles in a rock face and may one day be reported by a Thai archaeologist. Down in the 'jungle', meanwhile, the stunt team stayed back to film a last batch of elephant-shots and to cover remaining options. Rumours had spread like myths on set: had the film of the horse-and-elephant meeting been damaged by x-ray on the home journey? In fact, a virus had started to infect the remaining film rolls: to cover the risk of it, the animals had to gather for a final, quieter charge.

In Morocco, as the clothing trunks were packed up, a local cat had hidden itself in the cargo and was only discovered, asylum-seeking, at Reading in England ten days later. The local council threatened it with quarantine or death, but a radio-appeal from Rosemary led to its adoption, happily, by a Scandinavian rescuer. She named it, naturally, 'Alexander'. In Thailand, meanwhile, the elephants staged their last advance through the 'jungle'. At the final take, three of the leaders shook off their howdahs, pulled off their costumes, dislodged their mahouts and trotted off, unscripted, for a few days freedom in the gardens. It was a humbling reminder of their connivance, as if they knew when their role in film-history was over and they had had enough.

The long sarissas of the terrified Macedonian phalanx fail to deter a charging Indian war elephant.

Pre-production drawing for King Ptolemy's balcony in Alexandria.

Pre-production image of the streets and 'Tower of Babel' at Babylon.

15. VISUAL EFFECTS

The travelling circus on the outdoor locations was all very exciting, but it was only one part of a highly-planned strategy. Orson Welles' advice to a film-director was to choose a spot each morning on set, assert himself and start to film there, without worrying too much about alternatives. Oliver retained his visual freedom, but in his case it was backed by a meticulous grasp of the shots and angles which he needed.

For the big scenes, this group was backed by his weeks of work with the storyboard artist, Martin Asbury. Now in his early sixties, Martin is well used to rapid representations of complex action, step by step. He began his career as a strip-cartoon artist on newspapers, and then moved into films: before joining Oliver, he had been working on 'Troy', drawing out the action into no fewer than 4000 separate sketches. For Oliver, story-boards had never been important aids but the two battle-scenes, especially, needed prearranged depictions of men and camera-angles. A 'strip cartoon' helps to break down the action into pieces which can be allotted realistically into each day's schedule. On set, each sketch helps to position the crowds correctly for each take. With such a tight schedule (a third less than 'Troy's'), time-keeping was crucial.

In August, Martin had been flown to Los Angeles and set to work continuously. The Horse-Market scene with Bucephalas, the Gaugamela and Indian battles...: breaking them down, he would sometimes come up with angles which even Oliver had not imagined. For Gaugamela alone, he had to run off three to four hundred separate drawings. "Are you enjoying life in L.A.?" Oliver asked him after a week. Martin had not even had time to come out of his hotel-room. On 'Troy', he had seen the director Wolfgang Petersen alone for perhaps four minutes in all. On Alexander, he was meeting almost every day with Oliver, up to two hours at a time. Oliver's usual combination of flexibility and 'push' to a detailed vision struck Martin, too, in their workings.

The story-boards had a crucial destination: director of photography, Rodrigo Prieto. Day after day, Rodrigo would be constantly at the centre of the set, measuring light and never causing a technical fuss, yet the job of this important professional is central to the film's success. He had already worked with Oliver on three documentaries, including his one in Israel and Palestine in March 2002. Even there, nothing had seemed to ruffle him, so Oliver enlisted him for 'Alexander', knowing that Rodrigo had been nominated for an Oscar for his recent camera-work on 'Amores Perros' ('Tough Love'). Thailand, Morocco and ancient history were new ground altogether and a Director who wanted hand-held camera-shots, even among elephants, would never make it easy.

Outdoors, Rodrigo had to adjust to the ever-changing angles and strengths of each day's sun. In Morocco, the late afternoon shed a mauve light onto the battlefield's backdrops of hills and as the heat moderated, we all welcomed it as the 'magic hour'. It was a rough magic for Rodrigo who had to adapt the effect to the rest of the day's light. On horseback, we thought of the enemy as simply the enemy, deserving a lance through their middles, but Rodrigo had always to keep up consistent lighting, sunlight on the right cheek for the Persians, sunlight on the left cheek for the Macedonians. In his native Mexico, he had been used to sharply-changing daylight. But at any one time in Morocco he would be running five widely-spaced cameras in the field, planning their varying angles, deciding where, if at all, to back-light and how to cope with the dust. He could count on Ian Foster for brilliant shots of details, often hand-held, and after each take he would check the monitor-screens with Oliver and coordinate the next position or the next experiment.

The colour-codings of each section were crucially supported by the camera-equipment. Rodrigo had studied the same sources ('Le Mépris'; 'Intolerance') and had worked out a booklet of the film's changing tones. Each part of Oliver's complex colour-web was then planned round particular camera-filters and types of film. In Macedonia, the whites and primary colours were not filtered at all, whereas a polarising filter brought out the blue of the sky. At Gaugamela golden filtration brilliantly enhanced the desert dust. For the triumphal entry into Babylon, golden filtrations gave the right tone again, with a finer grain of film than was seen in the preceding battle-scenes. In the Bactrian fort, chocolate filters brought out the reds and earth tones of the costumes. The colouring of the Indian battle, of course, is the masterpiece: it was sharpened by film which retained the silvering. By this 'by-pass technique', the light becomes bright and the shadows much more black. When Alexander is wounded the camera-work is then slowed for the first time, until each second takes fifteen. The Macedonian army surge forwards, but as Alexander lies wounded, he and the Macedonians appear to see with fresh eyes. The cameras use an infra-red film: the green leaves shade into magenta, their skin into white and their ears into a hint of yellow. These wavelengths exist in daylight, but the participants briefly seem to catch them in a new vision. The infra-red film is very susceptible to temperature and the quantities needed for the scene had to be specially made.

These daring types of film then hit a practical problem: a virus began to show up on the filmed footage, suggesting that an entire batch had been infected on the way to Thailand. Had it been in one of the cans I had escorted on my way to cavalry service? The scale of the problem was still unknown as the team prepared for the final shooting at the site of the army 'mutiny'. Blue dots had been found on every eleventh frame of a batch which had already returned from the lab in Paris: could they be ironed out by the new technique of 'digital intermediation' on computer? The 'bleach by-pass' film was sufficiently challenging for insurers to have insisted that back-up film should be shot in a more usual form. How much uncontaminated film did Oliver have? He and Rodrigo set out on the final scenes of the army's 'return' with an Alexander who had just cracked an ankle-bone and cans of film which might be unusable and also unreplaceable.

Oliver Stone directs Rodrigo Prieto to a possible camera shot in the Moroccan hill above the theatre location.

Alexander's army climbs through the Hindu Kush (the Atlas mountains in Morocco, with artificial snow).

View through the Babylon palace as Alexander (Colin Farrell) prepares to meet the Persian king's daughter Stateira

Fortunately, enough of the footage was fine. Throughout, 'Alexander's' camera work is so memorable, avoiding the predictable, varying the colour and brilliantly using long-shots in a way which makes us feel spectators in such a special way. But right from the start, the weather played tricks. In Morocco, as the day for the entry into Babylon was cloudy, the crew decided to film the more sombre return of the battered army into Babylon, a scene from six years later. It takes a while to set up such a crowd-scene, whereupon the Moroccan sky changed. The bedraggled retreat was suddenly in bright sunshine after all, and later in the day, when the triumphal entry was reinstated, the clouds returned and threatened to dim it. It was for Rodrigo, somehow, to compensate.

Indoors, the artificial lighting could be just as difficult. Before Gaugamela, the scene in Alexander's campaign tent was too short of natural light under Jim Erickson's fabrics: Rodrigo had to ask for gaps in them so that the sunlight would play on Alexander and his battle-maps. Round the Bactrian fort, by contrast, the light in the mountains was so much cooler. Inside the council-chamber and the wedding-scene, its levels were too low, and so flame-throwers with torches were introduced to the partying in order to light up the proceedings. Overhead, Rodrigo had to install two thousand light bulbs, each of two hundred watts, on overhead wires in order to make the scenes work. Hard pressed for a solution, he had remembered the bright outdoor lighting of the 'guiernaldas', or fiestas, of his native Mexico. Even so, the system took three days to set up.

Back in Shepperton, the controlled, indoor setting of the Alexandrian library might seem an easier assignment. If the scene had been set outdoors it would have required a steady sunlight over its city-view, and as it is such a long scene, natural light would not have been controllable. Even so, the effect of a soft sun indoors needed 100,000 watts of lighting. Throughout, Rodrigo's 'gaffer' John Higgins kept a masterly control over lighting-levels. It was here that I watched the camera-team fixing the height and placing for each single shot of Anthony Hopkins's balcony scene. This setting has to be fixed and tested in advance, the business of two brothers, Malcolm and 'Chunky' Huse who somehow remained even-tempered and able to communicate calmly between viewpoints over their headphones. While seeing each shot through their lens, I realised how much of the set was irrelevant in each particular scene. Visitors might fasten their eye on a bent papyrus or a shiny statue, but the only 'eye' which would ever matter would be the camera-eye fixed on a restricted area by the Huse brothers and the steadiest of camera-operators, George Richmond. What they saw was all we would ever see on screen.

'All' of the built set, that is, for while Rodrigo and his team were filtering and focussing, a separate team of 'visual effects' experts were measuring the perspectives and sight-lines of every single shot in each scene so that simulated crowds and effects could be added later in post-production. Computer graphic simulation and animation from models have been the developing arts of big movies since the late 1970's. In 'Alexander', they allowed the breathtaking scale and city-vistas which transform the scenes of battle or urban living. While Hopkins narrated or our horses thundered through the desert, a skilled team of French and Californian experts quietly calculated how they would multiply the effect in subsequent months or add an entire city where only a blue screen cloth was hanging discretely behind Hopkins' presence.

Back in Paris, I visited the centre of 'visual effects', the offices of 'B.U.F.', in an ex-ministerial building in the smart Rue Roquepine . Here, presiding genius Pierre Buffin was guiding a team of up to eighty computer-artists, multiplying armies or Babylonian vistas in open-plan offices which looked like the dealing-room of a vast financial team. On set, the elegant Aurélia Abate and Sebastien Drouin had puzzled us warriors by their way of looking busy while apparently taking no strenuous exercise. Under the direction of John Scheele, who was usually near Oliver's side, they were actually logging every angle and line with which our action would be enhanced into a huge crowd effect. In 'Gladiator', audiences were amazed by the scale which new computer-techniques could bring to Rome's Coliseum or skyline. Since the early 1990's, the techniques have leaped forwards and 'Alexander' uses them in ways which make 'Gladiator' look disjointed.

At Gaugamela, we fought with up to 1500 men, but on October 1, 331BC, Alexander's army numbered at least 49,000, according to reliable evidence. To his officers' eyes, the Persian army numbered well over a million. He outnumbered Alexander and at Oliver's request, I sent sketches of the two armies' formations as their battle-orders were drawn up, opting for 170-200,000 as the Persians' total.

In Paris, it was a shock, and a revelation, to see such vast armies blackening the desert and the hillsides. In Morocco, our Call-sheets sometimes included '5 Shield Bearers, on blue screen: John Scheele". Such warriors with outstretched arms or weapons in their hands were photographed on set as 'stills' and then sent back to Paris for computer-modelling. Experts could even transfer these models' surface textures onto simulated figures. Their positioning was marked by carefully spaced dots, mapped in line after line, and then, the basic 'prototypes' were inserted into place by the thousand. To make them move, each small step had to be simulated one by one and run into a sequence. On seeing the first outlines, Colin had exclaimed, "I must have been a genius." On seeing the final battle lines, I could not contain a cry of amazement: I had never begun to imagine the scale, the chaos, the terror which Alexander's smaller army had confronted. My ideas of a big ancient battle have been changed for ever.

Oliver had met Sebastien in April 2002 while filming a commercial for telecommunications. B.U.F.'s previous films included the Matrix series and 'Batman and Robin' and by tendering for the job of 'Alexander', they won the huge task of inserting more than 200 'plates' into the live film. The Indian battle, meanwhile, was commissioned to M.P.C., in London, the major team behind 'Troy'. "Think of it," Aurélia and Sebastien explained to me, "as a process of layering: we build up the effect, starting in the deepest point of the film's background. We then work forwards layer by layer, like a sandwich - a French sandwich, with a special computer-mayonnaise." Unlike 'Lord of the Rings', 'Alexander' is using this technique on figures which have to be historical. It is much harder than applying it to mythical fakes.

As the Macedonians march along the river Euphrates in Babylon, the foreground is filled with living regiments, but the long files beyond are all a simulated crowd. On their flanks rise the facades of a computerised Babylon. The stepped holy ziggurat, or 'Tower of Babel', is another vast insertion: so are the city's traces of greenery, despite Roelfs's firm prejudice against palm-trees. Behind Anthony Hopkins stretches an inserted Alexandria which the actor himself never saw on his blue curtain. In front of Gladiator and me stretch a line of Bactrian cavalry which was never anticipated. Sometimes, a specially-photographed statue or relief was inserted from a museum-collection (the British Museum's new 'Queen of the Night' entered Babylon in this way). At others, there would be insertions of galloping horses or even, a soaring bird. In post-production, 'visual effects' inserted into the build-up to Gaugamela the necessary bird of good omen, the soaring eagle, bird of Zeus, whom the best ancient sources mention on the day. In a cold English winter, Aurélia and Sebastien had sketched and photographed while a male and female tawny eagle had been encouraged to flap their wings in front of air-currents, caused by a fan. Guided by their trainer the birds flapped almost too energetically. Back in Paris computer-graphics then simulated a body and steadier wings to go with the real bird's head. The result is a smoothly soaring eagle, signifying victory for the army whom visual effects had shown to be heavily outnumbered. The omen seems excellent, but as omens always are, it is a fake.

Director of photography Rodrigo Prieto.

Director (Oliver Stone) instructs Alexander (Colin Farrell) in the Babylon palace.

Director Oliver Stone checks with Persian king Darius (Raz Degan) in his chariot at Gaugamela.

16. History and Fiction

The contrasting battles in Morocco and Thailand frame the question of 'Alexander's' relation to history. They stand at either end of the spectrum which the film spans. The Gaugamela battle is correctly placed in Alexander's career and is based on the surviving ancient evidence, with a few inevitable compromises. In my view, it could be circulated to all schools, historians and universities for fruitful discussion of its sources and its adaptations (the camels charged, and several of the points in either line were changed). It gives a splendid impression of the units in action, the blood, the chaos: how much could anyone have seen when battle began? Above all, it gives a stunning sense of scale. No historian, certainly not I, has ever truly imagined the enormity of these battles, 50,000 men on Alexander's side against vastly more. The film shows us this scale for the first time. Archaeologists study ancient burial-grounds and survey the territories of Greek city-states, but most of these groups are tiny in comparison with these mobilised hordes of clashing males. The size of these armies is a distinctive fact about the ancient world, which was never matched again in Europe until the seventeenth century. We unmilitary modern 'professionals', I now realise, have lost an eye for the great mass-conflicts of the ancient world. Film restores what archaeology cannot.

In Thailand, by contrast, the battle was more symbolic, bringing together bits of history, shaping them to fit a dramatic plot and varying them to hold an audience's attention. Alexander's army did fight with elephants in India and even used axes and cutters on their trunks, but his biggest elephant battle was fought after crossing a river. It was a masterpiece in open country. Alexander never charged elephants in a jungle forest, and the elephants did not have Mogul decoration: they may not even have carried howdahs. Oliver placed his battle after the troops' refusal to march further east, whereas in fact, Alexander's big elephant-battle preceded it. In that battle, Bucephalas was indeed fatally wounded, but Alexander was not. His own big wound happened later at a siege in India and although his recovery was a highly emotional scene, it did not coincide with his decision to turn for home. That decision had already been taken.

Previous versions of the script had separated these facts correctly, and changes were not made in ignorance. Epic films about history have been much discussed for showing a 'Past Imperfect', but this neat label is the wrong one to apply. 'Perfect history' does not exist, nor was it ever Oliver's aim. His aim was an intense film-drama, not a documentary, and one source of this intensity is historical reference wherever he felt it appropriate.

The framework of 'Alexander's' life is a much more fascinating starting-point than an ignorant imagination of it. As a result, history is the film-drama's springboard and gives it force. But fiction is built into it too because characters have to speak lines for which there is no evidence. We cannot hear Alexander nowadays and we have next to no idea what he said. In the first century AD, Plutarch collected a few 'sayings' of Alexander, but they are sayings ascribed to him, and are probably not his actual words. It is interesting how high-minded they represent him as being, unlike modern minimalists' attacks on him. But they are not a tape recording and they are not the basis for a history-script.

So, a script-writer has to invent, and Oliver's script is a historical fiction. But it is a fiction exceptionally rooted in history, with strong interpretations of the person whom it represents. "Exceptionally rooted" is a just estimate. Among other ancient film-epics, 'Quo vadis?' was based on fiction and 'Ben Hur' or 'Gladiator' put fictional characters at their centre. In Alexander, by contrast, there are no fictional characters (though a dying soldier had to have a made-up name, 'Glaucus'). Above all, there is the film's backbone, the voice-over of Ptolemy. Ptolemy interprets his story too: he is prone to "look on the bright side": he is analytical in ways which the real Ptolemy's history (known only through later uses of it) was not. Like the real Ptolemy, the film's Ptolemy is economical with the truth, but the facts, dates and events which he describes are historical throughout. His existence gives Oliver's 'web' another dimension: the future (Alexandria) besides the past (Pella and Macedon) and Alexander's present, the bulk of the film. And old Ptolemy, in Hopkins's hands, is such a touching presence.

Not only are the characters historical: they play in the correct roles (Craterus the staunch Macedonian, Roxane the Bactrian bride). They also enrich scenes which are, for the most part, historically attested. The few exceptions are scenes like Alexander's conversation with Hephaestion on the balcony at Babylon or Alexander's weeping over the dead on the Gaugamela battlefield or the scene with Roxane after Hephaestion's death. They are dramatically powerful and indispensable to the plot, and certainly the characters concerned could have met and talked at such a moment: we do know Alexander visited the wounded after a battle and even tough Successor-kings would weep over the bodies of their rivals. However, early in the film Philip's visit to the caves below the Pella palace is certainly not historical: it is a memorable way of introducing the Greek myths which were Alexander's benchmark. These myths include the great stories of family conflict, mirroring, of course, Alexander's own in the film. On film it is splendid stuff, but it is extraordinarily unlikely that any archaeologist will ever prove Oliver's imagination to be 'correct' by finding such a cave under Pella's palace.

For the rest, it is worth knowing what is historically attested and accepted. Yes, Philip had several 'wives' (seven are known including non-Greek barbarians): yes, he was a great king, crushing Greek states to the south of his Greek kingdom. Yes, Alexander was brought up in Macedon and was taught, together with young friends, by the great thinker, Aristotle. Yes, Hephaestion was his greatest friend and surely a lover. Yes, Philip and Olympias quarrelled: yes, Philip remarried yet again and Attalus was credited with provocative remarks; yes, there was a brawl (we know about it from Plutarch's Life, based on earlier sources which only one loyal modern Greek historian has tried to wish away). Yes, Philip was murdered in a Macedonian theatre before Greek envoys by Pausanias, an assassin; yes, there was talk of Olympias's role in the murder. In Asia, yes, the Macedonians defeated a vast Persian army at Gaugamela and were welcomed into Babylon. Yes, the elderly Parmenion and his son Philotas were put to death. Yes, the army galloped after Scythians and conquered Bactria. Yes, Alexander married Roxane, daughter of Oxyartess, and survived a plot among his young pages. Yes, he invaded India and fought against elephants, and yes, Bucephalas died there. Eventually his army refused to march further east. Yes, one part of them had a disastrous return through the desert (which Ptolemy's history, like Oliver's Ptolemy, deliberately did not face up to in detail). Yes, Hephaestion died before Alexander, and his death made Alexander distraught. Yes, Alexander died at Babylon on June 10th 323 BC after his soldiers broke into his bedroom and staged an emotional march-past; yes, there was heavy rain. Yes, Roxane was pregnant at his death. Yes, Ptolemy eventually wrote a history while in Egypt, and Thais was the mother of three of his children. Yes, the eunuch Bagoas existed and (we are told) was one of Alexander's several lovers, although actually he appeared in 330 BC near the Caspian Sea, not 331 at Babylon.

Within this framework, there are events which were re-located and separate facts which were condensed. Sometimes a character lives on too long. Old Parmenion survives for three more years, seeing Roxane's wedding when in history, he was already dead. We do not know if Cassander was at Gaugamela and we are fairly sure that Antigonus the One-Eyed was not there, either, or in India. Neither he nor Cleitus murdered Parmenion. There were dramatic reasons for these liberties. Parmenion, old and cautious, needed a major actor and if the old and cautious voices kept changing in the film, their cumulative effect would be lost. By keeping him alive, the part grew and aspects in the dramatic web became more pronounced. By contrast, Oliver first gave a small but crucial part to the Persian queen and cast it, he hoped, with the French actress Jeanne Moreau. As the part was small, in the end she declined it and so the lines had to be redistributed. Antigonus, one-eyed, had a strong visual impact and so he was prolonged. As for Cassander, he had to be at the death scene with a shifty look, as a possible poisoner. He could not be introduced without a previous role.

There are also, inevitably, many omissions; not everything could be shown on separate sets at yet more expense. Instead, Ptolemy could allude to some of the important absentees. Everybody regretted that we could not show a siege, one of Alexander's great skills as a general: there simply was not time or money. Nor was there room to establish Darius's court and Persian culture in detail. Alexander's initial visit to Troy had to go too, because Ptolemy's voice-over must lead dramatically and directly to the great gamble, Gaugamela, the first scene in Asia in the film. Its up-front presence heightens its role, and a previous scene at Troy would blunt it. Oliver, of all people, knew what he he had had to omit, often from one of the previous drafts. If you regret something's absence, remember, as I must, that whatever else might go in would force something else to go out.

A constant problem was the history of Alexander's last three years. Robert Rossen's Alexander film never went into any of it. One way of including significant initiatives from this phase was to bring them forwards in time and attach them to an earlier scene with a suitable context. For instance, Alexander offers to pay his troops' debts and give wedding-presents to those troops who have married Oriental women. In history, he made this offer in Persia in 324 BC, but in the film he makes it in '327' BC, when marrying his own Oriental, Roxane. A separate scene could not be staged, so 'like attracted like', in a dramatically apt context. Alternatively, an event previously omitted is sometimes fitted to a later scene. The Persian King's family did indeed meet Alexander, and aspects of the meeting, as reported, were in the script (their mistaken bow to Hephaestion and Alexander's respect for them). But in history, the meeting happened in November 333 BC after Alexander's big victory at Issus. In the film, as Issus took second place to Gaugamela, the meeting was brought to the Babylon set (331 BC). So, too, Cleitus did save Alexander's life at a battle, but back in 334 BC. This saving was important dramatically for Cleitus's later murder and so it had to be moved to the one battle available, Gaugamela, three years later.

There are not too many of these relocations and none, I think, of which Oliver was unaware. However, the two most important are not simply constrained by a shortage of sets and time. One group is the sequence from the chasing of the Scythians to the entry into India, the other is from Ptolemy's Indian 'voice-over' to the decision to return home. To understand them, the film's sequence needs to be set briefly against history. In the film, we chase the Scythians, then go on to the wedding with Roxane: then comes the plot of Hermolaus and the pages: then, the plot of Philotas and the death of Parmenion: then, the entry into India, the light scene between Hephaestion and the monkeys, and then the dark scene of the Indian feast with resentment against Bagoas, followed by the murder of Cleitus. In history, the order is as follows; the plot of Philotas and the killing of Parmenion (330 BC); the rout of the Scythians (328 BC); the murder of Cleitus in Bactria (328 BC); the wedding to Roxane (early 327 BC); the Pages' Plot (327 BC); only then, the entry into India. There may or may not have been a meeting between Hephaestion and some monkeys, but Parmenion's death and Cleitus's murder have been postponed.

Why has Oliver rearranged these events? Dramatically, the aim is to underscore Roxane as a turning-point: in the film's sequence, it is the wedding to her which horrifies the older, narrower Macedonians (including Parmenion) and leads first to a plot by the young, then to one by the old. Historians are unsure why a plot had broken earlier and why Philotas was 'involved' in it (in 330 BC), but Oliver's transposition gives more emphasis to the major theme of Roxane. Cleitus's protest, too, gains force by following after the marriage, in a separate Indian setting which catches the audience afresh. But above all (as will emerge) this sequence allowed Oliver scope for all-important 'inter-cuts' to the 'parallel story' running in Alexander's drama, among events earlier in his life in Macedon.

The second transposition has similar reasons. In the film the troops refuse to go any further, Alexander threatens them and has the main mutineers put to death; then we have the Indian elephant battle and his fatal wound: then he recovers and in an emotional scene, announces the return home. In history, Alexander won a big victory over elephants on an Indian river plain; further on, the men refused to march East; he turned back and months

An impassioned Olympias (Angelina Jolie) against the mythical wall paintings of her bedroom at Pella.

Oliver Stone directs Olympias (Angelina Jolie) in a Macedonian moment.

Alexander (Colin Farrell) happily celebrates his wedding with veiled Roxane (Rosario Dawson).

King Philip (Val Kilmer) prepares to enter the fateful theatre at Aigai with his son Alexander (Colin Farrell) beside him.

later, down the river Indus, he was badly wounded while storming a town held by hostile Indians and jumping inside it from the walls. Only in 324 BC was there a separate mutiny when he tried to send his Macedonian veterans home: then he did order the ringleaders to be put to death. Again, the reasons for the changes here are space and drama. There was no room for a second mutiny, so an aspect of the later mutiny was transposed to the first one: it heightened its effect. There was no room, or money, for a second set and a siege of an Indian town, so the wounding of Alexander came up into the elephant-battle, together with the 'Shield of Achilles' on which (as in history) he was supported. But there is also a new drama; the wounding and the accompanying 'flash-back' are what made Alexander announce the decision to go home. In battle, we cavalrymen were (supposed to be) hanging back, because among other things, we had refused to follow Alexander in the previous mutiny scene. In history, the hesitations in the troops during warfare occurred months *after* the turning for home. By taking the troops demand to 'return' in two stages – one denied by Alexander, one accepted – Oliver heightened a coherent drama.

It is important to be straight, here: these transposed sequences are not history. They are not true to it and by changing events around they are not historical. Some film-makers (not Oliver) claim that historians cannot know things for sure: their sources, surely, are biased or non-existent, and just look how historians disagree (at times Dale Dye inclines to this view). But even among our poorly-documented sources for Alexander, this general approach is wrong. We know of a framework, bits of 'what happened when', where Alexander went (although the exact routes are often uncertain), what battles he fought, what officers he used. Our sources agree on much (but not all) of this framework and therefore, there is evidence for it. By changing the order, a scriptwriter ceases to be historical. He may claim, instead, to be true to the 'essence', but there is no objective 'essence' in history: it is the claimant's own interpretation. If the interpretation is putting events into the wrong sequences, it will not be historical; it may, however, be dramatic.

Historians certainly do not want to deny that their histories are subjective. Of course they are, like good film-making, but unlike film-making, they are at risk to evidence, and the evidence can sometimes refute them or let them down. In defence of their own creative art, film-makers (but not Oliver) sometimes claim that "all history is rhetorical". But history is not only 'rhetorical': it is based on evidence. Nor, more desperately, is "all historical truth subjective" or "all truth subjective". For if that statement is true, its truth is 'subjective' too : why should others believe it? In my view, film-makers about the past would save themselves reams of wastepaper in drafts, scripts and dollar bills if they submitted themselves first to a 'Fact Camp' with evidence to devour instead of breakfast. What they need is 'Historians Incorporated'; it would greatly improve many films about past events and save a fortune in preliminary spending. It was a late chance that a historian worked on 'Alexander' and it was luck that the Director was historically minded too.

Like film-makers, historians have to be selective, but time and money oblige film-makers to be much more selective. Like historians, film-makers interpret events and are subjective, but unlike historians, they are not controlled by evidence and their estimate of it. Historians explicitly analyse the past in terms of abstract concepts, the modern categories

163

which we apply back to it: film-makers have to show such concepts (class-conflict, demography, gender-relations) through specific scenes, not abstract words. But film-makers do have one advantage: they can easily show multiple points of view, different reactions to words and events, by their camera-work and inserted dialogue, and they do so more economically than historians. What, then, is Oliver's interpretation of Alexander?

Stone's Alexander is interpreted by Ptolemy, by the dialogue and camera-angles and by the underlying web of the plot and its parallel stories. His Alexander is certainly a hero, and a hero with a vision. He is consciously bringing change to an East which, in places, strikes him as being primitive (the speech to Hephaestion on the Babylon balcony). Babylon certainly is not primitive: it is a great old civilisation, but there are tribes and peoples who are, and one function of the new Alexandrias is to tame them and bring them urban life (Alexander did try to settle nomads in towns, as farmers; four centuries later, the Greek Plutarch certainly interpreted Alexandrias in this way: nowadays, the minimalists and post-colonialists reject any such notion, but that is only their view of the moment and personally, I can accept that a Macedonian, a patron of Greek culture, did indeed want to spread centres of Greek civilisation across Asia). In an expansive mood, his friend Ptolemy even recalls him as a "new Prometheus – a friend to man..." That is Ptolemy's licence. Unlike the older officers and Cassander, Alexander wants respect for Persians and Iranians, by one of whom (despite them) he plans to father a son and heir. As he sickens, the 'vision' becomes more extreme: "a library in each Alexandria". (This notion is rather a neat one, as we do not know who or what first inspired Ptolemy to found a huge library in Alexandria. The current scholarly guess is a pupil of Aristotle, but Alexander had studied with Aristotle too...) He had been wanting to reach the edge of the world and though the troops turned back in the East, he is still wanting to reach such an edge in the West (this plan may well be genuine; in my view, he believed he had found the world's outer Ocean in the south; he was sending explorers to investigate it in the north and at the end of his life, he was very probably after it, too, in the West).

This Alexander is certainly not the Alexander of modern minimalists, but their idea of him has had to discard, or evade, bits of evidence which go against it; such is the rhetoric of 'realism' or 'pragmatism'. One cohort of scholars in the 1980's even ground Alexander's 'greatness' down into a 'dance with Death' and a near-paranoid obsession with plotting and a willingness to invent 'conspiracies' against threatening contemporaries. He was not a visionary (they assert) but he was a pragmatist who used Orientals only as a 'counterweight' against his own unreliable men: he was even misrepresented as a 'Macedonian barbarian', not as a Greek. This tendentious 'realism' never convinced Oliver or his actors or, quite separately, me, and key points of it can be refuted by evidence. In contrast the Stone Alexander is certainly not a 'dreamer', but he does have a vision. He is not fighting to the end of the world in order to go on terrorizing everybody else and to prove his virility while covered in blood.

On the other hand, there is a real beast in him which even old Ptolemy cannot hide. A 'friend to man' – but what about the families of the dead in India? What about Cleitus (The truth is - "I wanted to...")? Or the rage with his army before turning back? Or with

King Ptolemy (Anthony Hopkins), the great survivor, on his balcony in Alexandria, some forty years after Alexander's death.

The prophet Aristander (Tim Pigott Smith) prepares to pray at the bull sacrifice before Gaugamela with Alexander (Colin Farrell) whose helmet is held by his page Hermolaus (David Leon).

Party scenes at the Indian feast, shortly before the murder of Cleitus.

King Philip (Val Kilmer) stands and attacks his son Alexander for his insults to Attalus at his wedding.

Hephaestion's doctor? Stone's Alexander is certainly not a white-wash. His Macedonia, correctly, is Greek and correctly, Alexander has both male and female lovers (ancient sources describe Bagoas as one, and assume, sometimes state, that sex was also part of his love for his 'Patroclus', Hephaestion: Alexander also ended up with three wives at once). He drinks more than enough: he alarms his officers and they do not share his 'vision'. But he is not an Alexander stamped down into dust (with only his generalship exempt) because nowadays we hate great men and share a moral revulsion from killing in an unprovoked war. Once people submitted, or were defeated, Alexander had no wish to go on persecuting or killing them. Nor was the India which he entered an India at peace, without internecine war: by conquering it, he ended existing localised wars, as the Romans did later in so much of their empire. Tens of thousands of Indians and Iranians joined his army in the attempt. Stone's 'Alexander' is seen from more than one angle, and audiences will be wary of taking Ptolemy's viewpoint entirely as Oliver's own.

Above all, there is the tightly-planned web of 'parallel stories'. Here, Oliver's sense of drama transformed previous attempts at a script. His script's stage-directions help to explain the implied psychology. As a boy, Alexander is caught between his mother and his father, his mother who "loves too much" and "makes him weak", and his father who urges him to sacrifice things and "be strong". He defends his mother to his father, then his father to his mother. Even when taming Bucephalas, he "pauses at an apex between his parents, as if, for a moment, his aching heart could bring them together." These two poles are then explored by the artful placing of each 'parallel story' or flashback.

At Pella, Olympias urges him to marry a Macedonian, have a child and become Philip's established heir: he is 19 years old. We remember, ten years later, when Alexander marries Roxane, a barbarian, which Olympias was not, but one with a slight look of dark haired Olympias and a shared taste for snake-ornaments. To mark this new turn, events (plots and so forth) are moved around so as to follow it as cause. After a second letter from Olympias, we cut, significantly, to memories of the quarrel with Attalus back in Macedon. An earlier wedding (Philip's), an earlier quarrel... In Babylon's palace, Alexander had asked old Parmenion to "forgive my anger and my pride... they too blind me." ("Parmenion is a little bewildered...") But next, Parmenion is killed and then, in India, Cleitus is killed by Alexander's "anger". Roxane, his wife, is now hardening, even more than Olympias (at the Indian banquet it is a nice touch that the Bactrian Roxane is now protesting about the Indians around her). Cleitus's murder revives the 'parallel story' of Philip's murder in Alexander's past. In India, the troops then refuse to go on, and Alexander, proud and angry again, has the ringleaders killed. He embarks on the Indian battle, but he is badly wounded and at last, the "memories he has blocked" spin before him, his blaming of Olympias for his father's murder. When Alexander recovers, he sets aside his pride and gives the army what it had wanted: a return home. Significantly, Val Kilmer (Philip) is seen in a tableau beyond the army, approving his son.

But there is still the dark presence of his mother, Olympias. Her complicity in Philip's murder has been all but established by the flash-back to the event while Alexander lay wounded in India. Back in Babylon, Hephaestion had been the one who understood: "I

167

wonder sometimes... if it's not your mother you run from... ('Alexander looks aghast')".
Now, Hephaestion dies, the only one who could speak directly to him, and worse, Alexander blames Roxane, the woman who has become so much harder than his own mother. (There is no evidence that Roxane actually poisoned Hephaestion, but Oliver introduced the suspicion, to my mind very effectively). Without Hephaestion, we see Alexander drinking and the rivalry with the mythical heroes ebbing away. Yet again, his mother writes to him and we hear Alexander softly responding. "Yes... come to Babylon... I want you... your only loving son..." On the surface of the wine he seems to see 'his MOTHER'S heightened expression of fear...'. Her face is now wreathed in snakes, a real Fury. He drinks it, cries out suddenly in a sharp pain and goes on to die: had Cassander put something into his drink? We never know...

The 'parallel story' in Macedon is so artfully placed, especially from Bactria onwards, and the placing explains the re-location of events. Olympias's warnings must precede the marriage with Roxane; the Cleitus affair must lead on to memories of Philip's death; the memories of its aftermath and Olympias' role then lead to Alexander's regaining his troops' admiration by announcing the return home. But (as in the myths on the cave-walls below Pella) Alexander's mother is still pulling at him: will she now come to Babylon? This implied drama gives the film an unusual intensity. It is not reductionist, as if it is the only drama about Alexander or the only real story: from the start, Oliver's exchanges with Thomas Schühly had guarded against such a travesty. The rivalry with the heroes, the beast (the Titans) in us and him, his impulsiveness, his generalship, his thinking: all these strands are there too. But by inter-cutting, a psychology runs through the story. It is quite untrue that people from the past 'cannot' (as a matter of *principle*) be 'psychoanalysed'. Every time we attribute them a motive, we do so. What is true is that as a matter of *fact*, we cannot psychoanalyse them in any clinical (possibly mythical) sense: we do not have the living relationship on which such clinical analysis is based. In my view, the influence of family tensions was true and important long before Freud, and the need for love is universal among human beings wherever and whenever they live, in Africa, in California, in the nineteenth century, in ours, in fourth-century Macedon, in Bactria and elsewhere. In principle, then, such an analysis of Alexander might be right; the fact is, we do not know. We know that his mother was capable of ordering murders, of behaving courageously and of lavishly worshipping the gods. She did write to Alexander, but we have no genuine letters. Did Alexander really run from her, fall for Roxane because she resembled her and end up with somebody even harder? As for Philip, it is highly likely that Alexander was sensitive about his father's great achievements. In antiquity, historians thought so, although the evidence is not contemporary with Alexander himself. As he became more convinced that Zeus was his divine father, was Philip somehow 'disowned'? Oliver avoided this particular line and preferred, with a touch of drama, to have Alexander winning, at last, his father's approval. But before Alexander himself had a son, he died, with the boy still unborn.

Stone's 'Alexander' is certainly not a loosely-constructed film: it is the result of fifteen years' thinking and refining. As a historian, I do find that the drama forces us to remember that emotions and responses existed at that time, and that our evidence simply has not passed them on. "There was suspicion", our best source, Arrian, writes, "for Alexander towards Philip when Philip took Eurydice as his wife and dishonoured Olympias". But what did Alexander feel and say, as he must have done? "He was already not far from Babylon with his forces drawn up for battle, and the Babylonians came to meet him in a mass, with their priests and rulers, each of them bringing gifts..." What ever did Alexander feel? A film-script has to invent, but it reminds historians of what is missing when their texts are such matter-of-fact statements and proper nouns.

Apart from its web of psychology, Stone's Alexander is nearest to an Alexander he had not read, the Alexander of one of the greatest scholars of this period. In 1931, Ulrich Wilcken, then professor in Berlin, judged that "The greatest difficulty of all lies in Alexander's own personality. Not only was his character very complex and made up of apparently irreconcilable opposites, but there was in him a superhuman quality; and genius is never quite capable of explanation. The riddle of his life cannot be solved by resort to reason alone, for alongside a clear and sober intellect, he had in him much that was non-rational. To regard him simply as a coolly calculating politician is to overlook the romantic and mystical traits in his nature. A judgement of his achievements is rendered more puzzling by the fact that a premature death carried him off in the middle of his creative activity. We have only beginnings, and in no single instance was the last word spoken". Among full length dramas on film, 'Alexander' is the first.

To a delighted army, the recovered Alexander (Colin Farrell) announces the return home, flanked by Craterus, Antigonus, Leonnatus, Nearchus and Perdiccas in India.